ANOTHER NOW

BY THE SAME AUTHOR

Talking to My Daughter: A Brief History of Capitalism (2017)

Adults in the Room: My Battle with Europe's Deep Establishment (2017)

And the Weak Suffer What They Must?: Europe, Austerity and the Threat to Global Stability (2016)

The Global Minotaur: America, Europe and the Future of the Global Economy (2011)

YANIS VAROUFAKIS

Another Now

Dispatches from an Alternative Present

THE BODLEY HEAD
LONDON

3 5 7 9 10 8 6 4 2

The Bodley Head, an imprint of Vintage,
20 Vauxhall Bridge Road,
London SW1V 2SA

The Bodley Head is part of the Penguin Random House group of companies
whose addresses can be found at global.penguinrandomhouse.com

Penguin
Random House
UK

First published in the UK by The Bodley Head in 2020

www.vintage-books.co.uk

A CIP catalogue record for this book is available from the British Library

Hardback ISBN 9781847925633
Trade paperback ISBN 9781847925640

Typeset in 12.25 pt/16 pt Bulmer MT Std
by Integra Software Services Pvt. Ltd, Pondicherry

Printed and bound in Great Britain by Clays Ltd, Elcograf S.p.A.

Penguin Random House is committed to a sustainable future for
our business, our readers and our planet. This book is made from
Forest Stewardship Council® certified paper.

For Danaë,
without whom Another Now would be unimaginable
and This Now intolerable

Foreword

A year ago today we buried Iris in a red and black coffin. Red for the revolutionary fire constantly blazing in her belly. And black to remind us, as she kept doing, of the irreducible dark side in us all.

Iris's funeral was as she would have wanted it, save for Eva's absence. The tributes provided a fitting encomium for my extraordinary friend but the words washed over me. Some twenty years had passed since I had last seen Iris and Eva together. They had been sitting on Iris's patio, Eva holding her usual glass of Pinot Grigio, Iris scolding her in tirades punctuated only by mouthfuls of chilled vodka. *Why on earth did Iris ever take Eva under her wing?* I recall wondering.

For a woman who could never have conceived of a good market, a noble war or an unjust strike, it was an improbable friendship. Eva was a recovering investment banker turned true-blue, dry, academic economist. Far from having a winning personality, if anything she exemplified Oscar Wilde's definition of the cynic – she who knows everything about prices but nothing about values. 'And I'm not even sure she has a *clue* about prices!' Iris once said teasingly in her presence. Nonetheless, as Iris's casket was being lowered into the ground, Eva's absence weighed heavily.

With Iris and Eva gone, Costa was the only other one left of our old gang. On the day Iris died I had messaged him twice, using an old number I still had. To no avail. Resigned to endure the funeral without him, I was surprised when I glimpsed him there. He was not easy to spot, a solitary figure leaning against a plane tree, watching from a distance as Iris descended to her resting place.

Once the mourners began slowly to disperse, I approached him, and his face thankfully brightened up. Though his youthful cheerfulness was all but gone, his eyes still glimmered with his characteristic blend of brilliance and sentimentality. But as we talked he seemed harried and close to paranoia, focused terribly on 'the diary' and how important it was that it should not fall into 'the wrong hands'. It was then that I realized Iris had been in cahoots with him before she had summoned me to the hospice, two weeks before her body gave in to the cancer.

Iris's summons arrived in late June 2035, jolting me out of a two-decade-long seclusion. The last time I had seen either of them was in August 2015 as I was passing through Brighton for one last time, my life in the early stages of an unrelated meltdown. As soon as I entered her room in the hospice, Iris struggled to sit up, determined to muster all her fading energy to receive me. Dismissing any preliminaries, she pointed to a diary sitting on her bedside table and gestured for me to take it. 'It comes with a directive and an injunction,' she whispered.

The directive was unequivocal. I was to focus on the 'dispatches' in the diary and use them 'to open people's eyes to possibilities they are incapable of imagining unaided'. As for the injunction, she made me promise I would not reveal any of the 'technical details' in it. 'In due course you will know what I mean,' she muttered. Finally, in a bid to lighten the atmosphere, she told me with typical bluntness and bossiness, 'Get stuck in to it the moment I'm dead and buried.' Eager not to burden her further, I held her hand and made the promise she had demanded.

Little did I know that 'in due course' meant Costa appearing at her funeral to deliver my instructions, which he did breathlessly in a quiet corner of the graveyard car park. When reading Iris's diary, he said, I had to take precautions against the corporates: 'Iris wanted you to have her diary. She wanted our story told so that the world understands there *is* an alternative. But I know she warned you of the one, strict condition: none of the detailed information in the diary regarding my technologies should fall into their hands. Tell me that you understand!'

I reassured him that I did. He stared into my eyes to confirm my sincerity. 'We had it wrong all these years, Yango,' he said eventually. 'We knew that everything about us was being commodified. That everything we did and said was being captured and sold on. But what we had *not* realized was that the process of digitizing everything about us was proletarianizing everyone, including the bosses. Think about it, Yango. Think about it.'

It had been a while since I had found myself on the receiving end of such an outburst, but it seemed somehow appropriate, given that we had just laid to rest the greatest agitator of revolutionary politics I had ever known.

'What does it mean to be a proletarian, really?' Costa continued, without waiting for a reply. 'Let me tell you. From bitter experience. It means you are a cog in a process of production that relies on what you do and think while excluding you from being anything but its product. It means the end of sovereignty, the conversion of all experiential value into exchange value, the final defeat of autonomy.'

Without a clue as to why he was telling me all this, I agreed.

'This is why I am *still* here, Yango. Why I stayed behind. To prevent our final defeat at those bastards' hands. I can't stop them inventing it for themselves but I'll be damned if I let them grab mine and use it to squeeze the last drop of humanity out of us all.'

Satisfied that I had been adequately briefed, Costa took a device from his backpack and placed it firmly in my hands. 'It's a dampening field device. Idiot proof,' he said with a hint of contempt. He showed me how to switch it on to prevent the 'bastards' from gaining access to Iris's diary.

Hoping to catch up properly after all these years, I suggested dinner or at least a drink. Costa simply stared into my eyes, gave me a tight hug and left without looking back.

Watching him walk away, his eyes fixed on the ground, the lyrics of a melancholy Greek song I had learned as a teenager sprang to mind.

> Late last night I saw a friend wandering
> A hobgoblin-like relic on a motorbike
> Stray dogs chasing after him
> Through deserted streets

I was reminded in turn of a solemn middle-aged visitor in a shabby raincoat who had stopped at our home in Athens one winter night to give my father some tattered old communist literature. 'We shared a police cell in 1946,' Dad whispered sadly when his comrade later left into the cold, wet night.

But Costa's words reminded me of someone else: Sam, the main character in an old sci-fi flick. A miner slaving away on the dark side of the moon, Sam is driven mad when he discovers that he is one of many clones that have been created by his company as a supply of cheap, disposable workers, and that he has been duped with implanted memories into believing his long-dead family are still alive back on earth, awaiting his return. Science fiction is the archaeology of the future, a leftist philosopher once said. It is now on the verge of offering the best documentary of our present.

Friends' funerals usually leave me numb but functional. But on returning from the cemetery after Iris's, I struggled to steal back into my present. The leather-bound diary that Iris wanted me to have lay tantalizingly on the desk. I ignored it for the rest of the day, but in the early hours of the following morning I surrendered. I sat at the desk and opened its heavy cover.

Two red arrows filled my vision as my hybrid-reality contact lenses detected audio-visual content in the diary and kicked in. Instinctively I gestured to switch off my haptic interface and slammed the book shut. Costa had explicitly instructed me to set up the dampening field device before opening the diary. Chastened by my failure to do so, I went to fetch it. Only once the device was on the desk, humming away reassuringly, was I able to delve into Iris's memories in that rarest of conditions – privacy.

It took nine days and nights to go through the diary, taking in Iris's handwritten remembrances as well as all the audio-visual content embedded in its pages. Halfway through I stumbled upon the extraordinary events of 2025 involving her and Costa and Eva, and came to understand why Iris was so keen for their story to be told. Once I had been through it all, for two long months I struggled to fend off the urge to do what

I always do when upset or destabilized: to write. Instead, I used those sixty days to digest the material properly, to read, to watch and to listen to it again and again and again.

The tale contained in Iris's diary shook me deeply. Iris knew this would be so, just as she knew that I would find it impossible not to write it up, for better or for worse. The book you are about to read, dear reader, took another nine and a half months to write. And so it is, exactly a year after we buried Iris in that red and black coffin, that I am now ready, with a single keystroke, to deliver the manuscript to her publisher. If only there was some way she could tell me what I have missed.

The bulk of the diary, and the majority of what follows, is taken up with a series of dialogues. It was these intellectual and political debates that concerned Iris, far more than the events that led to them. In an attempt to do full justice to my friends' ideas and points of view, I have found it necessary to recount these debates as if I had been witness to them myself, pretending to inhabit a past from which I was mostly absent, fleshing out conversations I never participated in. In the process, I have necessarily imputed thoughts and feelings to Iris, Eva and Costa that are the product of my imagination – but only because I felt such additions were essential to conveying the essence of their experiences, of who these good people truly were. For all my liberties, and failures, I apologize profusely and happily.

Yango Varo, 10.05 a.m.
Saturday 28 July 2036

1

Modernity's Vanquished

Iris

Iris and I met in the dystopia that was English university life. We were both miserable, she at Sussex, me at Essex. 'Sex with a prefix,' we used to joke. It was early in 1982 that our paths first crossed – at the London School of Economics, in one of the countless meetings convened in those days by left-wing activists for the purpose of fighting Thatcherism. After two hours of tedious speakers huffing and puffing on the podium, Iris rose to make her contribution. She was magnificent.

'While listening to the previous speakers,' she said in a resolute but playful tone, 'I was thinking to myself, *Give me Maggie Thatcher any time!*' Evidently relishing the expressions of dismay from the audience, she continued: 'Unlike you, my friends, Maggie gets it. We live in a revolutionary moment. The post-war class-war armistice is over. If we want to defend the weak, we can't be defensive. We need to advocate as she does: out with the old system, in with a brand new one. Not Maggie's dystopic one, but a brand new one nevertheless. You lot are bandaging corpses while Thatcher is digging graves. If I were condemned to choose between you and her, I would choose her any time. However monstrous she may be, she can at least be subverted!'

It was my baptism with Iris's fiery spirit. But while her words resonated strongly with many of us, they also guaranteed her ostracism. Radicals tend to take exception at being denounced as banal. When once I accused her of being a lone wolf rather than a believer in solidarity, she replied proudly and without a scintilla of irony, 'That's me!'

As the years passed, Iris's natural fondness for alienating those who broadly agreed with her world view grew in proportion to society's adoption of its opposite. Thatcher's greatest triumph, in her opinion, was that she had made it impossible to imagine anyone doing anything unless there was something in it for them. Contrarian to the bone, Iris was appalled and energized by the realization that everyone was at it, coveting unfettered power where they could get it – including in public meetings denouncing Thatcher, the City and the more refined forms of greed. Iris was thus a passionate feminist who could not stand most feminists, considering them privileged actors with a fear of sexual freedom and a habit of speaking on behalf of, and over, those who ought to be leading the movement against patriarchy. She was a lesbian who also had sex with men out of 'a penchant for solidarity with the defective sex and a predilection for pissing off lesbians'. She was a Marxist who despised most Marxists for using Marx's emancipatory narrative to abuse other comrades, build their own power base, gain positions of influence, bed impressionable students, eventually take control of the politburo and throw anyone who questioned them into the gulag. Above all else, Iris was a thinking radical's thinking radical. Energetic and brilliant one moment, vexing and maddening the next.

That evening at the London School of Economics we struck up a conversation, possibly because I was the only one in the audience to applaud her. A few months later, on a dreary December night in 1982, Iris called to say that she was helping plan a mass women's rally outside some RAF base against the deployment of American cruise missiles targeting eastern Europe. Could I turn up to support them? I arrived at Greenham Common late the following day. In the pouring rain 30,000 women tried to join hands around the base in the face of determined opposition by the police. Just as I decided that it would be impossible to find Iris in the mayhem I spotted her on the cold, muddy ground, two women kneeling by her side holding a handkerchief to a bleeding gash on her forehead. 'From an overzealous defender of the realm,' she told me grinning proudly.

A young-looking twenty-eight-year-old, Iris was at that point three years into a social anthropology lectureship, having returned from field work in Africa, where she had compiled lexicons and written down the grammar of the languages spoken by two Cameroonian tribes. Several years her junior, I was struggling with my own PhD on mathematical models, which Iris dismissed, not without some justification, as 'fine exercises in logical-positivist masturbation'. Over the five years that followed, in between our university duties, we would join multiple doomed causes together – the 1984-5 miners' strike and the 1986-7 Wapping dispute the most demoralizing of them. One hundred and five weeks, in aggregate, of picketing, fundraising and being on the wrong side of history should either have pushed us apart or forged an unbreakable friendship.

I remember visiting her one day in hospital in 1987, after mounted police had trampled all over her outside Rupert Murdoch's gleaming Wapping site, and asking if the fear of physical harm had ever brought her close to giving up. Iris replied that when you join a good struggle you learn to live life in near proximity to giving up without ever actually doing so. No, her only regret was that we were putting up such a splendid fight in defence of communities that deserved defending but in pursuit of causes that screamed 'anachronism'. 'Why can't we bring the country to its knees to demand clean energy and a free press, instead of defending dirty coal-fired power stations and the male trade union bosses of a right-wing newspaper?'

Defeat could never sully Iris's sweet delight in fighting against the odds. No rout could dampen her enthusiasm – 'No good cause is ever lost,' she liked to say – only the fear that we were lions being sent to the battlefields by donkeys. She distinguished between two types of self-proclaimed progressive leaders. Those defending privileges bestowed upon them by the dying post-war order and the others, the more radical ones, bent on replacing the prevailing order with a different but equally oppressive patriarchy. It was only as I was driving her home to Brighton from hospital that same evening that I realized how haunted she was by this conviction.

'OK, let's say we are the vanguard. But the vanguard for bloody what?' Breaking a long silence, Iris's outburst startled me. 'Mark my words. The moment our comrades get a whiff of power they'll sacrifice every principle they ever held. And those of us who remain dissidents will be demonized, or more likely ridiculed.'

By the time I pulled up outside her house, she was looking sullen and beaten, the first time I'd ever seen her that way. 'I can't stand for this,' she announced. 'I just won't.' And then she got out of the car.

A few months later, in the early summer of 1987, Margaret Thatcher won her third successive general election. The following day Iris resigned her lectureship. She also stopped attending political meetings. Neither university nor the picket lines held any of the allure that had kept her going. Falling back on a modest bequest that she had received when she was in her late teens from a sweet old man, a hereditary peer who loved to scandalize polite society by referring to himself as the queen of queers, she had the luxury of being able to drop out. 'For some reason, he saw me as a muse he had to provide for, god bless him.' Oddly, her explanation seemed to make perfect sense and I made no further enquiries.

When I asked her reasons for the double exit, she answered by producing two pieces of paper. One was a circular from Sussex University in which the students were referred to as customers. 'If that's what they are, they are the sort who are always wrong,' she commented. The second piece of paper was an internal Labour Party memo referring to the infamous Clause IV of its constitution, the party's long-standing commitment to 'secure for the workers by hand or by brain the full fruits of their industry ... upon the basis of the common ownership of the means of production, distribution and exchange, and the best obtainable system of popular administration and control of each industry or service'. Ever since 1959, there had been those within the party who sought to have this commitment to nationalization removed, but the trade unions had resisted. Skilled at reading the writing on the wall, Iris knew what the memo foretold. In the wake of their recent defeats, the trade union bosses were preparing to drop, even as an idle vision, the dream of common ownership over the utilities, the factories, the railways and the various high streets and marketplaces where commerce unfolds. It was game over, she thought.

'Nineteen eighty-seven is as good a year as any for these trade unions to die out and follow our universities into oblivion. And for me to return to my tapestries.' Which is precisely what she did.

Iris had picked up the art of knitting elaborate tapestries during her time in Cameroon. Her instructors had been the villagers with whom she lodged while documenting their languages. Here the norm was for the women to work all day in the fields, while the men stayed at home to cook, clean, look after the children and knit. She had been taught tapestry making by men whose social status hinged on the beauty of their handiwork and whose pattern-less knitting techniques liberated her imagination. What resulted were stunning depictions of intricate, and often lewd scenes, drawing on African, European, Indian and Japanese imagery.

Iris took Thatcher's triumph as her cue to withdraw to her upstairs sunroom and dedicate herself to an art form that defied polite society's familiar categories. Of course, within a couple of years they had started selling at respectable prices in galleries in Geneva and London, even at auction. As I write these lines, one of the first tapestries she made that summer, featuring a sumo wrestler performing an erotic dance in Buckingham Palace, hangs above my desk, its woollen surface fraying and yellowing a little, but its irreverent power undiminished after forty-eight years.

In the evenings, however, it was business as usual at Iris's Brighton terrace. Her home remained the sanctuary it always had been for our circle of friends and hangers-on, who would gather at her house most evenings for drinks and debate and to be thrilled, reprimanded and cheered by Iris in equal measure. For years thereafter, she behaved like a constructed contradiction: the gregarious recluse of Brighton who passionately embraced anyone in need of her support while meticulously refraining from commitment either to person or to cause. Until, that is, Eva appeared on the scene twenty-five years later.

Eva

Eva moved in next door to Iris on a summer's afternoon in 2012. The twenty-eight-year-old Californian arrived in a taxi, straight from Gatwick, with her five-year-old son Thomas and three large suitcases in tow. Minutes later Iris was knocking assertively on her front door to invite her over for a welcoming glass of wine and to meet whoever happened to be visiting later that evening.

Having put Thomas to sleep and set up the remote child monitor on her phone, Eva popped round. Introducing herself to the gathered, she explained that she had come to Brighton from the United States to take up her first-ever lectureship – at Sussex University. A year or so previously she had earned an economics PhD from Princeton whose title, 'Three Essays on Game Theoretical Models of Evolutionary Psychology', would give Iris boundless opportunites to mock her viciously over the years. The mockery, however, hid a growing empathy due in part to the realization that Eva was on the run: that both her academic career as an economist and her passage to England were elements of a broader escape. What Iris could never have imagined back then was how far Eva's escape would eventually take her thirteen years later, in the closing days of 2025.

Chance and a talent for mathematics were central to Eva's story. In 2006, as a twenty-two-year-old graduate in theoretical physics from Stanford, she had followed her privileged ilk to the riches of Wall Street, first as an intern at Goldman Sachs then as a ridiculously remunerated financial engineer at Lehman Brothers, the financial world's *Titanic*. When Lehman hit its iceberg in the autumn of 2008, Eva abandoned not just the sinking ship but the whole racket. After a few months of clearing her head, she enrolled at Princeton's graduate school of economics in early 2009, determined to lose herself in abstract, fully mathematized theory, seeking refuge in the economic sermons that once steadied her hand as a financier.

Soon after arriving at Princeton, she discovered she was pregnant. Iris made a mental note of how meticulously Eva avoided any mention of the father, proceeding swiftly to recount the nine months she lived in a peculiar isolation, her mind and body in two vastly differing realms: while one surfed the most extreme abstractions, the other, with her baby growing inside it, provided the most powerful awareness of her own materiality she had ever known.

For the first two years of Thomas's life, Eva saw hardly anyone except for her baby and, occasionally, her academic supervisor. Iris imagined her as a cross between an East Coast pietà and a traumatized lieutenant who retreats from the butchery of the battlefield into the monastery that had blessed his generals' holy massacres. 'She ran away from Wall Street to hide in Princeton,' I recall Iris whispering to me, 'to hone the theories that underpinned her financial crimes at Lehman's.'

And in 2012, with her doctorate scarcely under her belt, Eva retreated again, this time leaving her country and its more lucrative university system for Britain and the University of

Sussex. She was not yet thirty and already Eva's life resembled a steady evacuation.

Iris and Eva came from different intellectual and moral universes but, as they eventually came to recognize, it was their shared sense of paradox and trauma that provided the underpinnings of their most peculiar bond. Iris, the great practitioner and theorist of collective action, operated as a one-woman army. Eva, an unswerving individualist, felt keenly her abandonment and the absence of human bonds in her life. While neither cared to admit to it, their separate paradoxes mirrored one another. So too their traumas.

Eva had been born in 1984, the year of the miners' strike. The failure of that strike was Iris's Waterloo, sealing her life as a permanent defeat. But what the miners' strike had been to Iris, Lehman's collapse had been to Eva. And just as in 1984 we realized painfully that we would live the rest of our days as history's losers, so in 2008 Eva saw history erupt on her own doorstep with the same soul-destroying, optimism-sapping force. Each had experienced the shocking epiphany that their world was no more. It would prove the force that dragged them, despite strenuous resistance, down the path to an odd but solid friendship.

That summer's night in 2012, when Eva crossed Iris's threshold for the first time, the mood turned from jolly to prickly rather abruptly. Iris had invited Eva out of a sense of neighbourliness, feminist solidarity with a single mother struggling alone in a new country and curiosity. But as soon as Eva mentioned her past as a banker, Iris was unable to help herself.

'Bankers are only good at sucking the oxygen out of society,' Iris declared. 'They divert extraordinary resources to the spivs, while lending either far too much or far too little but never, ever to those who either need the money or who plan to do useful things with it. So,' she told Eva condescendingly, 'on balance it is a good thing that you switched from destroying people's lives on a planetary scale to polluting the mind of England's young with lectures on the efficiency of financial markets.'

Eva lacked Iris's enchanting insolence but was no pushover.

'People trade through markets for the same reason they do business with the laws of gravity,' she shot back. 'Are you proposing to replace those too? Surely equipping the young with the skills they need to navigate the world they inhabit is preferable to polluting their minds with pointless utopias?'

'My dear Eva,' Iris replied, 'universities are not about imparting skills. They are about producing flexible minions dying to do as they are told. You are there to manufacture young people willing – desperate – to be moulded to their future bosses' priorities. And the first step is to get them to swallow without question your faith that markets are as natural as gravity and profit the only worthy aspiration.'

Back and forth they went, with Eva matching every one of Iris's insults with a passive-aggressive rejoinder.

'I don't deny the harm done by financial markets and profiteering,' replied Eva at one point, 'but grubby money-making is never capable of damaging humanity as much as your collectivist dreams have done. You mean well but you're paving the way to the next gulag archipelago. You oppose commodification. It's my job to persuade my students that it's humanity's greatest hope!'

Uncharacteristically, Iris allowed Eva to get away with this lazy riposte. The young American had clearly hit a nerve, no doubt the same one that had prompted Iris's withdrawal from academia and political activism all those years ago. Terminally frustrated with the Left's authoritarianism, Iris now found herself – for the first time ever – yearning for a dose of Eva's impoverished libertarianism. So instead of taking one of at least a dozen easy shots available to her, Iris simply smiled, raised her glass and, retreating into Shakespeare as she so often did when feeling mischievous, pompously welcomed Eva to England, to 'this precious isle set in a silver sea'. It was the end of their first confrontation.

A short while later, Eva excused herself, saying Thomas had been alone for too long, and said goodnight.

'Poor girl, she stands no chance,' Iris scribbled in her diary that night. 'This England never did, nor never shall, lie at the proud foot of a conqueror.'

Eva was already getting under her skin.

Costa

Costa parachuted into our circle long before Eva. I first came across him at King's College London in 1989, at yet another tedious Thatcher-bashing meeting. An accomplished engineer, born in Greece, trained in Germany and then working in Amsterdam, Costa had been invited to give a left-wing perspective on what was soon to become the new economy. His prescient speech stood not a chance with that audience.

In 1989 British leftists were up in arms against Thatcher's notorious poll tax and its impending passage from Scotland to England and Wales. Even the most technically savvy in the audience still worked on clunky Amstrads with floppy disks and no Internet connection. What were they to make of Costa's passionate appeal to combat the establishment with 'digital messaging, financial engineering and artificial intelligence'?

'Science-fiction fantasies are an indulgence when people are hurting, mate,' shouted one member of the audience.

'Capitalism and science fiction share one thing,' he replied coolly. 'They trade in future assets using fictitious currency. Even if these tools are still in the realm of science fiction, they are our best defence. Believe me, given half a chance the powerful will wage an all-out war against the rest of us using these high-tech weapons. We must deploy them first if we want to stand any chance of defending ourselves.'

His nonchalance in the face of the crowd's hostility brought back memories of my first encounter with Iris, seven years previously. A brief exchange afterwards was all it took to establish that we shared far too much. This we blamed on our common background in the island of Crete. We left the meeting together and ended up at a shabby Indian restaurant a few blocks south of the Thames where we continued talking until after midnight.

A somewhat shy man of roughly my years, Costa had been both a tech evangelist and a tech heretic since his adolescence in Archanes, a small village south of Heraklion. After high school, like many Greeks of our generation, he fled to 'Europe'. In 1979 he enrolled at Stuttgart University on an engineering degree. Immediately upon graduating, five long years later, he was recruited by Dornier to design missile guidance software. For three years his fascination with the engineering challenges clashed with his conscience. By 1988 his conscience had won and Costa resigned. Within a month he landed his dream job with Cornea PLC, a small company based in Amsterdam that employed him to design bionic implants to aid the blind.

Costa had been working at Cornea for only a year when we met but, once again, disillusionment had already set in. The corporate profit drive was no less deadly in the health than in the arms industry, he had discovered. Only a few months ago he had designed an upgrade to a microchip that massively enhanced an implant's capacity, which he proudly reported to the senior management. In response he had received a memo that congratulated him on the new device's technical performance only to inform him that his upgraded chip would nonetheless be mothballed. Cornea intended to continue selling its grossly inferior chip indefinitely.

When Costa protested, his line manager had explained the company's rationale. Their main competitor was struggling to improve upon Cornea's existing implant, which cost little and was selling well. They had no need for an expensive upgrade to stay ahead of the competition. But by simply leaking the information that Cornea had one waiting in the wings, their competitors would be dissuaded from investing any further, while avoiding the possibility that they might reverse-engineer the new chip if it were released.

'My bosses understand,' he explained, 'that the best way to profit is first to establish a monopoly and then strategically to starve the market of the product they have monopolized.'

The thought of blind people being denied the help his invention could provide made him furious. The company's reasons for withholding it and its power to do so revolted him. These two emotions would eventually propel him to leave the company and embark on what would turn out to be a professional roller-coaster ride in the years that followed.

Listening to him talk that night, I had a wild idea. Costa should be introduced to Iris. It was a risky move. Iris could be relied upon to treat him abysmally, if only to test his nerve. But I had a feeling it might lead somewhere interesting.

'Come and meet the Miss Havisham of our failed revolution,' I urged him. Eventually he was persuaded, and the following evening I drove him to Brighton.

Had Costa been made of sterner stuff, I would have worried less. But he seemed fragile and unprepared for Iris's eccentric ferocity. Thankfully, my concerns proved badly amiss. Iris took an instant liking to Costa. She recognized in him a rare quality: a willingness to absorb others' suffering to halt its transmission and the nastiness it breeds. The technological universe he inhabited was wholly alien to her, and she eagerly listened to the insights he shared from it. When he left that night to catch the last train back to London, Iris's natural cynicism remained at bay.

'Despite his hilarious Graeco-German accent, your new friend is a living reminder of William Morris,' she said excitedly. 'Something deep inside him detests the dehumanizing ways in which new technologies are produced. If only the humans producing them were allowed to craft them like artisans – not like machines breeding machines. And yet this doesn't stop him from appreciating the beauty and the virtues that they afford.'

Costa provided Iris with a window on to a new world. It was clear from the start that she found the view both mesmerizing and disconcerting. And so began a friendship that would last the rest of their lives.

With the arrival of Eva in our circle many years later, I realize now that three people had come together who had each in their different ways been lured in and then defeated by modernity: Iris by a long string of dispiriting leftist calamities, from the tragedy that befell her continental heroes Rosa Luxemburg and Aleksandra Kollontai to the triumph of Thatcher's Britain; Eva by the weapons of mass financial destruction and 'riskless risk' that she herself had once peddled; Costa by his badly misplaced faith in the digital revolution's emancipatory powers.

Each ended up in self-imposed isolation. Iris in her Brighton terrace. Eva in English academia. Costa, as we shall see, in his lab. But through their friendship and Costa's reaction to his particular predicament, their isolation was transformed into something like its very opposite – at least for a few, devastatingly interesting months in the second half of 2025.

2

Another Now

Deliverance

Costa's reaction to his defeat began in the early 1990s. It was to prove consequential.

Quietly, he started using Cornea's facilities to carry out personal research projects, taking advantage of the company's hands-off attitude, aimed at encouraging their engineers to explore their skills and creativity to the full. From the start, his main interest was brain implants. He would provide a new enhancement or design just often enough to keep his employer happy, but all of his major innovations – of which there were many – he kept entirely to himself.

Towards the end of that decade, however, he could not help but have his attention diverted by something else: the skyrocketing value of high-tech stocks, including Cornea's. Convinced that they would soon crash-land, he used up his savings to short every high-tech share he could. And when the dot-com bubble eventually burst in 2001, Costa made a very tidy sum, enough to earn him sufficient freedom to take a risk and leave the company. Immediately he resigned from Cornea and explained to Iris that he was moving to San Francisco. His visits would be less frequent. But this was the break he had been looking for: an opportunity to set himself up in Silicon Valley.

Costa took a job with a company developing digital implants intended to minimize pain by non-pharmaceutical means. But his hopes that Silicon Valley might be different were soon dashed when, once again, an update of his was put on hold by the company in order to extend the shelf life of existing products. So Costa returned to his earlier strategy of using company facilities to work secretly on his own projects.

Meanwhile, the stock market rapidly recovered – so rapidly that Costa grew suspicious. History was about to repeat itself. When a couple of years later a bank contacted him with an offer of a 120 per cent mortgage for any sum for any property in the Bay Area, he trusted his instincts – already vindicated by one stock market crash – and ploughed his entire savings into shorting any bank that traded in American mortgage-backed derivatives. In other words, almost the entire Western banking system. And so, when finance had its near-death experience in October of 2008, ending Eva's career at Lehman, Costa found himself sitting on a multi-million-dollar nest egg.

'Free at last in the valley of broken dreams' was how he announced his changed circumstances in a handwritten letter to Iris, who placed it in a special section of her diary dedicated to Costa's more momentous missives. 'Now I can do something useful with all the gadgets I have created but lacked the time and resources to develop,' he waxed hopefully.

The day after Barack Obama moved into the White House, Costa resigned, rented a large space in downtown San Francisco and set to work to put all of his secret technological innovations to work.

The Lydian ring revisited

Costa had been introduced to the fable of Gyges as a teenager by his high-school scripture teacher, a Cretan version of

Quentin Crisp who eventually made a name for himself as a decent poet. Struggling in his lab to find humanist uses for his technologies, Gyges' ring gave Costa an idea.

According to myth, Gyges was a poor shepherd in the ancient kingdom of Lydia who one day chanced upon a magic ring. By rotating the ring on his finger, he could make himself invisible. So he walked into the palace, seduced the queen, murdered the king and installed himself as ruler of Lydia. In *The Republic*, Plato has Socrates ask: if you discovered such a ring, would it be rational *not* to use it to do as you please? Costa remembered Socrates' answer well: anyone who uses the power of the ring to get what he wants enslaves himself to his own appetites. Happiness, and not just morality, hinges on one's capacity *not* to use the ring's exorbitant power.

Costa was not romantic enough to expect people to heed Socrates' advice. He knew that almost everyone would succumb to the temptation to use the ring pretty much as Gyges had done. But he had long thought that a device devastatingly more powerful than the ring would give people pause and, in so doing, shake them out of their self-defeating sense of self. Three years after Costa isolated himself in his downtown San Francisco laboratory, the tale of Gyges took on new and urgent significance when the idea of precisely such a device came to him.

It happened when Costa was visiting a colleague at their home in Seattle. There, he observed the resident teenager playing a multiplayer video game with thousands of other participants, presumably young people also sitting in their bedrooms and appearing on each other's screens in avatar form. Costa was instinctively appalled but also fascinated by the discovery of these emergent communities.

The ultimate goal of the Silicon Valley's gaming corporations, he realized – and indeed the Holy Grail of big tech as a whole – was a device that replaces the hit-or-miss offerings of real life with a sufficiently realistic virtual reality machine tailoring its offering to each individual's desires. At the same time, humans continue to crave connection with one another: interacting with a machine is fine so long as the fantasy is a shared one. Killing an avatar, knowing a real person lies behind it, is far more satisfactory than bumping off a purely computer-generated space invader. This need to see and be seen explains why those games that allow the player to share the action with millions of others, while remaining cocooned in their living room, are in such demand.

The problem with humans, Costa surmised, is the same in real life as in digital games: we crave the company of other minds, whose validation is meaningful because they are beyond our control even while control of them is precisely what we seek. When they do things we do not want them to do, we get upset. But the moment we control them fully, their approval gives us no pleasure. It is ever so hard to learn to appreciate that the pleasure to be had from such control is illusory, especially since people are prepared to sacrifice almost everything in its pursuit. Costa's audacious idea would resolve the conundrum once and for all. The device he planned to build, his Freedom Machine as he playfully called it, would let millions of people inhabit the same virtual world but experience their mutual interactions differently. It would fashion not merely a universe of bliss but a multiverse of infinite, simultaneous, overlapping pleasures.

Imagine the feat of letting Jack experience hiking with Jill while, at the same time, Jill is attending a Shakespeare play alongside Jack – or even with someone else! A machine that lets all of us experience – and share – our desires all at once. Freedom at last, not only from scarcity but also from what other people do to us, expect of us, or want from us. Suddenly, others would do, think and act in total sync with our dreams, hopes and aspirations. Constraints would become obsolete – a distant reminder of a primitive existence. Our dilemmas gone, all trade-offs eradicated, boundless satisfaction at our fingertips.

Such infinite power to shape the world in one's image exceeded the ancient mythologists' imagination and made Gyges' ring seem puny and crude. If Socrates hoped he could persuade us to forgo Gyges' ring on the grounds that its power would wreck our lives, surely he stood no chance of dissuading us from entering such a multiverse of unimpeded bliss? Unless, Costa thought, the price of entering the world of the Freedom Machine was that you could never leave it.

The power of for ever

Every genius relies on a questionable assumption. Costa relied on two of them. His first was that most people would ultimately decline the opportunity to live the rest of their lives in his Freedom Machine. His second was that this recoiling would be fundamentally liberating to them.

Costa knew, of course, that we would all be terribly tempted to enter the Freedom Machine. That was its whole point. The harder it was to resist, the greater the liberation it would grant those who turned it down. But would *anyone* turn it down? Ultimately, Costa wanted to believe, we all would. For ever is a long time to be spent in any state of bliss, let alone in an illusion created by a machine. Even fools, radical hedonists and the clinically depressed would recoil from surrendering their minds to a machine for ever. Faced with the ultimate, really-existing Gyges' ring, he had no doubt we would shock ourselves by saying no. And the moment we turned down the offer of a perfect multiverse, he postulated, we would be thrown into an existential spin, resulting in a state of sheer lucidity. Suddenly, we would grasp the truth that Socrates wanted us to understand: the greatest slavery is that of our own appetites. Merely by existing, the Freedom Machine would give us a priceless shot at the most liberating of epiphanies: that there is more to life than indulging desires and eliminating pain.

Costa's life changed the moment this line of thought resulted in the following conviction: Gyges' ring had not worked for Socrates because it was not powerful enough and, more importantly, it was not actually real. It remained a myth, a thought experiment. But what if Costa could adapt and develop his various inventions in such a way as to build a functional Freedom Machine, demonstrate that it worked as advertised and then give people the entirely real option of giving themselves to it for ever? What if people did indeed turn it down? Not only would Costa have gone one better than Socrates, he would have discovered a way to undermine the very basis of capitalism: people's readiness to think of themselves as consumers.

Traditionally, the Left chastised capitalism for manufacturing in us desires that capitalism was bound to frustrate. Costa agreed with this critique but wanted to take it a step further: even if capitalism were to deliver on its promises, satisfying every consumerist whim it instils in us, it would only succeed in destroying the possibility of true freedom and, with it, of the good life – *eudaimonia* as his ancient forebears called it. The Freedom Machine would reveal once and for all how empty, soul-destroying and joyless the satisfactions on offer are once we have been transformed from humans into consumers. In Costa's hopelessly romantic mind, we would come to see that a state of permanent bliss of the type that capitalism promises is in fact a form of purgatory. Nothing liberates us from a monopolist more readily than the revelation that we don't want his wares. The question was: could Costa actually build the Freedom Machine?

HALPEVAM

Costa spent the first three years of his freedom from salaried labour reviewing and improving upon his earlier work: not just bionic eyes and painkilling implants but a host of devices that fuse directly with the brain and nervous system in order to control our senses.

By 2012, he had already constructed a highly complex and effective human–machine interface, which in a letter to Iris he described as 'a fascinating solution to a hitherto undiscovered problem'. When later that year his idea for the Freedom Machine took shape, he was overcome with the stunning realization that, suitably developed, his gadgets could indeed become the backbone of a working prototype.

Modesty prohibited him from referring to his prototype as the Freedom Machine. He opted instead for the technical term HALPEVAM: Heuristic ALgorithmic Pleasure and Experiential VAlue Maximizer. Later, when extraordinary circumstances compelled him to explain it to Iris and Eva,

Costa introduced HALPEVAM as the opposite of the misanthropic machines in *The Matrix*. In that classic film from 1999, networked machines manufactured a virtual reality into which they sought to enslave every human mind on the planet while exploiting their bodies as a source of thermal energy for their soulless empire. HALPEVAM would, by contrast, be humanity's ultimate slave.

In the early days of HALPEVAM's development, Costa was slowed down by a theoretical problem. What form would time take inside HALPEVAM's multiverse? Specifically, how would time's passage be experienced if one had infinite experiences all at once? Surely a life of boundless, overlapping experiences need last no more than a nanosecond? Time would be infinitely wide but infinitesimally brief. Had he discovered the secret of embedding an eternal heaven within a vanishingly short lifetime? These questions paralysed him for a few weeks. It took another, more pressing problem for him to get unstuck.

For HALPEVAM to work as a liberator, it was essential that there was no reason for people to fear it might brainwash them – an entirely understandable concern when deciding whether or not to plug into a machine capable of messing with one's head. For if people were to turn down the opportunity to enter HALPEVAM's multiverse for ever out of a legitimate fear that they might be brainwashed, they would not be turning it down for the reason Costa wanted them to. It was, therefore, absolutely critical that the experiences HALPEVAM offered each user were generated wholly by that person's own desires and nothing else. If there was any possibility that the machine might operate according to its programmer's agenda or that it might be able to instil alien desires into the person who used it, then that person would effectively have become a slave to the machine and the entire project would be undermined. This became HALPEVAM's prime directive: a ban hardwired into it that prevented the machine from inputting into its users' minds *anything* that they did not bring with them when joining in its digital utopia.

The challenge then became how to capture a complete and accurate picture of the user's desires, passions, beliefs, whims and predilections. A snapshot of our brains' contents at the moment we join it would not be enough. HALPEVAM would somehow have to tap into accurate, unbiased, complete information about our entire experiences before that point as well. The only way such a harvest could be possible, Costa concluded, was if our very experiences leave behind them some form of permanent, physical record. Like all scientific prodigies, Costa first imagined the existence of this record – a trail or wake we leave behind us made up of quanta of experience – before setting out to construct the instruments that might detect it. And to help himself believe in its existence, he gave it a name: CREST – Cerebral Recursive Engram Subatomic Trail.

Almost eight years had passed in pursuit of CREST when in 2020 the world went into lockdown. Costa would hardly have noticed, isolated as he was in his lab, had it not been for the sudden influx of invitations from the few friends he maintained any contact with to chat with him via various web-based applications. At first, he resisted all electronic visitations. But then, in April 2020, his instruments began to detect CREST. Bursting with excitement, and despite his obsession with secrecy, he skyped the only person he trusted to share his delight with: Iris.

'Think of it as the quantum wake of our lived lives slipping out of our evolving engrams,' he explained. 'It sounds complex, I know, but really it couldn't be simpler!'

'You mean something like a subatomic river of life?' Iris asked.

'Yes, precisely,' he said. 'A river you can never step out of twice.'

'Either you have entirely lost your marbles,' she replied, 'or you think I'm the world's most gullible fool. Perhaps both. Either way, I'm delighted to see you haven't changed a bit.'

By the summer of 2021 Costa had developed a method for not only tapping into CREST but also for reconstructing the experiences it contained, providing HALPEVAM with the raw material it needed to generate a near-infinite multiverse of user realities. 'I am on the CREST of bliss,' his cryptic text message to Iris read on the happy day that he plugged himself into it for the first time.

For safety, Costa programmed HALPEVAM to detach his mind from CREST almost as soon as it was connected. But for the few milliseconds he inhabited its world, he experienced a truly dizzying form of rapture, a glimpse into a life beyond anyone's wildest dreams. That vanishingly small moment was the headiest experience imaginable.

Afterwards, it took hours to take in what had just happened. But as soon as Costa was able to accept the incredible fact of what he had created, its terrifying implications choked him with anxiety: what if the corporates got wind of what he'd made? How on earth would he stop anyone from hacking into or even stealing his invention? What if big tech got its hands on CREST, the ultimate source of data about each and every one of us?

Panicking, Costa immediately focused all his talents and energy on erecting the strongest possible firewall around his invention. Thus was created Cerberus, a formidable security device whose bizarre malfunction would change everything.

Cerberus

When Iris tenderly entrusted her diary to me in the days before her passing, she made me swear that I would honour a second prime directive, one that Costa had intended just for me.

'Our dear Costa has become paranoid,' she explained. 'But then again, didn't Joseph Heller point out that just because you're paranoid doesn't mean they aren't out to get you?'

My prime directive was clear: I was not to divulge any of the rich details in her diary that might help those eager to tap into CREST break Costa's Cerberus code. A blessing in the form of a constraint, I thought, as it liberated me from having to account in any substantial detail for technicalities well beyond my comprehension. Suffice to say that Costa devised a system whereby access to HALPEVAM and to CREST relied on a long PIN derived from his own DNA sequence but constantly evolving along a stochastic path in sync with his own engrams. Even if hackers were to get hold of his DNA, it would be impossible to break Costa's code unless the hackers also had access to Costa's thoughts in real time. In theory, Costa had rendered CREST untappable by anyone except himself.

For the next three years, Costa lived on the verge of an anxiety attack, feverishly developing and refining HALPEVAM to the point when he could truthfully alert the world that a multiverse of bliss was available to all. Then, on Saturday 25 January 2025, events intruded with their usual ferocity. Costa spent that evening with some Greek friends celebrating an anniversary that meant much to them and nothing to the rest of the world. Upon returning to his lab, his heart sank when he saw there had been a break-in. And then it plummeted when he discovered how close the intruders had come to tapping CREST.

Watching his account of that night, recorded in Iris's diary, I finally appreciated the significance of what he'd said to me at Iris's funeral. Costa had dedicated his life to preventing 'the bastards', as he called them, from stealing access to CREST in order to create a private market for emotions, memories, ideas – in other words, turning HALPEVAM into its opposite and fashioning humanity's ultimate slavery. Costa discovered that the intruders had used remote brainwave scanning technology to monitor his real-time thoughts and DNA they had lifted from his toothbrush to come within mere minutes of decoding his PIN. They had failed only because the walls of the underground bar where Costa and his mates had gathered were thick enough to interfere with the transmission.

Energized by this near disaster, Costa began to build Cerberus. Named after the mythical two-headed beast guarding Hades, the realm of the dead, this improved security system had two new features. One was an upgrade to the code so that access to CREST was only possible if Costa's mind was actively wishing it. The other was a doomsday feature, inspired by the crazed nuclear war strategy of Mutually Assured Destruction that the Pentagon had toyed with in the 1950s: the creation of a bomb so vast it would destroy all life on earth if the enemy unleashed a nuclear warhead, thus deterring them from ever doing so. So too, Costa set out to deter big tech from tapping into CREST by means of a device powerful enough to destroy CREST once and for all in the event of unauthorized entry.

By early April, a Cerberus prototype was ready for testing. It would involve the destruction of a single strand of CREST's subatomic trail in total and pristine isolation within a special chamber. The trick was to choose exactly the right amount. Too much might damage or even destroy CREST as a whole. Too little would fail to demonstrate Cerberus' power.

'I appreciate the agony,' he wrote to Iris, 'of the first medical researchers seeking the right dosage for the smallpox vaccine. To protect CREST from big tech's greed, it appears I must risk destroying it.'

But given that he could not un-discover CREST, he felt he had no choice. The date of Cerberus' first scheduled test was set for 7 April 2025. As it drew closer, Costa's belief in his chosen path grew only firmer.

Diploma

Uncreased are the vistas of tedious landscapes. But, as the unexpected results of Cerberus' test so amply demonstrated, it is the convoluted, folded spaces where genius, intrigue and wonder are to be found.

The idea of a fold in space–time, allowing instantaneous communication with or travel to another time and place via a wormhole, was first explained to us by Einstein. But fascination with folds and their power runs deep in our myths.

When King Proetus of Argos decided to dispense with young Bellerophon, whom his wife had unsuccessfully tried to seduce, myth has it that he devised what should have been the perfect crime. Proetus summoned Bellerophon and gave him a vital top-secret mission. The young man's task was to hand-deliver a letter to Ioabates, King of Lycia and Proetus's father-in-law.

'Under no circumstances should you show the letter to anyone or read it yourself,' he ordered Bellerophon. 'Were you to do so, your own safety and that of our kingdom would be jeopardized.'

Eager to please his king, the young man gave his word that he would do as he instructed and under no circumstances open the letter. Satisfied, Proetus took out a papyrus and wrote on it his deadly instructions to the recipient: 'Kill the bearer of this missive. If you fail to trust me and he lives, your kingdom is in peril.'

Proetus then folded it carefully twice, sealed it, and handed the *diploma* – the Greek word for a piece of paper folded twice – to Bellerophon, then sent him on his way.

But by folding the letter, Proetus unwittingly caused the undried ink to smudge, obscuring some of the words, so that when Ioabates unfolded the papyrus, all he could make out from it was the following: 'If you … kill the bearer of this missive … your kingdom is in peril.' Thus, Bellerophon was spared – and not until Einstein reinvented our view of the cosmos did a double fold have as much of an impact on Western civilization's collective consciousness.

By the end of the day on 7 April 2025, Cerberus appeared to have passed its test with flying colours. The subatomic trail had been fully scrambled without any discernible damage to CREST as a whole. Immensely satisfied with the preliminary results, Costa programmed HALPEVAM to run a complete diagnostic overnight, locked the door to his lab and went to bed, where for the first time in years he fell into a deep and unbroken sleep.

On the morning of 8 April 2025, a Tuesday it was, he woke up in a fine mood, hopeful that Cerberus would soon be operational and that his wild scheme to liberate people might actually become a reality. With his mug of coffee still in his hand, he began reading the diagnostic data HALPEVAM had produced overnight.

The data made no sense. Not that it was incomprehensible. On the contrary, it was completely legible and of a structure that he instantly recognized. In fact, the closer he looked, the more obvious it became. Reading through the stream of digits and machine-language printouts, he realized that what he was looking at was a message, encoded yes, but ultimately written in plain English and apparently addressed to him. He set to work deciphering it.

'Who is this? And what do you want?' it began.

These were the precise questions he wanted answers to himself! Where on earth had this message come from? And who was the sender?

Further tests provided the unfathomable but irrefutable answer that the message was coming from his exact same location, in San Francisco, sent by a person with his very own DNA. For a while he wondered whether he had gone mad, or if he had somehow written this message himself and forgotten. Had HALPEVAM taken on a life of its own, perhaps? But no, the tests showed that, impossibly, the message had arrived during the night, while he was asleep and the lab was locked. It had been written by him, in this very place, on the night of 7 April 2025, and yet he knew for a fact from the security log that the lab had not been opened until this morning, and as far he was concerned he had just enjoyed the best night's sleep he'd had in years. It was as if the message had come from an alternative reality: from an alternative version of himself inhabiting another now.

Though it took him almost a month of further tests and experimentation, it was the myth of Proetus, Bellerophon and the *diploma* that eventually gave Costa the clue he needed to resolve the puzzle. Somehow, incredibly, the energy involved in testing Cerberus and scrambling CREST had been enough to create a tiny fold in space–time, opening up an Einstein-Rosen wormhole, just as those scientists had predicted. Though no wider in diameter than a subatomic particle, this minuscule duct was sufficient to allow a stream of data to flow from one side to the other.

Unlike Bellerophon's *diploma*, which resulted in his marriage to a Lycian princess with whom he lived happily ever after, Costa's precipitated a stream of messages that threw his already strained life into total turmoil. By the end of June Costa had worked out how to communicate with the person writing to him from the Other Now. Using 1970s batch-file messaging technology, so old it required only minuscule bandwidth, he was managing to send messages back through the wormhole, and receive replies, of several thousand characters – one at a time.

Once the communication was established, Costa gave himself over to it utterly. All thought of HALPEVAM's intended purpose was swept aside. Thanks to the irksome time lag between messages, progress was slow, but within less than four weeks, a remarkably detailed picture of this person – an alternative version of himself – and the world he inhabited was coming into view.

By comparing notes backwards in time, Costa and Kosti (the name he had chosen for his self in the Other Now) concluded that their personal experiences and historical trajectories were identical but only up to a very specific point, at which their memories branched off, leading them to two starkly different realities. Until that point, historically, politically, socially and economically, the Other Now was identical to our own – and yet from that point onwards, drastic differences became apparent. The moment when divergence set in could be pinned down to the autumn of 2008 – at almost exactly the moment of the great financial crash.

As he poured over Kosti's dispatches, Costa's initial shock at the mere fact of their existence was replaced with one of shock at what they contained. Costa's long-standing assessment of the crash of 2008 was that it had been too good a crisis to waste, and yet waste it we did. It could have been used to transform society radically. Instead, we not only rebuilt the world as it had been before but, by bailing out the banks and making the working people pay off the debt, we had doubled down on it, instituting a global regime in which, effectively, political and economic power had been handed over wholesale to the most bankrupt of bankers. Costa had always believed that an alternative had been available to us. A road we never took. Now, it seemed, he had Kosti's dispatches to prove it.

Slowed down by the obligation to answer Kosti's own queries regarding our sad reality, Costa took care to ask only the most pressing of questions. What had Kosti meant when he mentioned that the corporation he worked for had no boss? What did he mean when he said there were no longer any banks? That no one owned land or paid taxes? What had been the catalysts for such a momentous transformation in such a short space of time? With every reply received, Costa built up a treasure trove of information about the Other Now. Meticulously he recorded his correspondence with Kosti, compiling and editing it into a single continuous dialogue in preparation for the day when he would be able to share all that he had discovered with Iris.

3

Corpo-Syndicalism

No bosses, no wages, no problem

'OK, here is how we do things,' began Kosti's account of the corporation in which he worked. 'No one tells anyone what to do. We choose freely the persons or teams that we want to work with and also how much time to devote to competing projects. Everything in our company is in flux. Staff move about, new teams are formed, older projects die, new undertakings are concocted. No bosses to order anyone around. Spontaneous order and personal responsibility overcome the fear of chaos.'

This constant flux was a design feature of corporate life in the Other Now, Kosti explained. When hierarchies are used to match people with particular roles and teams, the result is clumsy, inefficient, oppressive. Status anxiety and the need to satisfy one's superiors make full transparency impossible. People are kept in the dark about the relative attractiveness or drawbacks of working with particular managers or colleagues, how happy or dysfunctional teams are, how rewarding or boring different projects. Hierarchies simply perpetuate and expand themselves, resulting in a terrible mismatch between a person's standing and what they actually contribute. Even the hierarchy's great advantage, of ensuring that all posts are staffed at all times, is a hidden loss.

Under the flat management model, Kosti acknowledged, there are frequent gaps. But the fact that they are observable to all makes them useful. When people notice an empty spot where David's desk used to be on the sixth floor, and then discover on the company's intranet that he moved to the fourth floor to work with Tammy, Dick and Harriet, everybody learns something important about the value of the work being done in that nook on the fourth floor. With people voting freely with their feet, an ongoing collective assessment takes place of each project's relative value. If unpredictability is the price of staff autonomy, it is a small one to pay, Kosti reported.

'But surely there must be a hierarchy when it comes to recruitment?' Costa asked. 'Surely there are menial tasks that no one would *choose* to perform?'

'No, no hierarchy is involved at any level – not even in recruitment or the assignment of shitty chores,' replied Kosti. New staff are taken on informally, he explained, without the need for a personnel department. If Tammy and David need, say, a graphic designer to work with them but cannot find one within the firm, they post a notice on the intranet announcing themselves as the initial search committee, inviting others to join them if they wish. Once assembled, the impromptu committee places an ad on the company's public website to solicit applications. The committee then compiles a shortlist and conducts interviews, which anyone in the company is entitled to witness either remotely, via the intranet, or in person. Finally, Tammy, David and the rest of the search team post their recommendation, and anyone who wants to is able to cast a vote either against or in favour of their chosen candidate.

The same process is used, no matter the job, including for secretarial or run-of-the-mill accounting positions for example. New staff are recruited on the understanding that, once in the company, no one can force them to be secretaries or accountants. And indeed, Kosti explained, it is often the case that people recruited for these tasks eventually branch out into more creative roles in a way that no hierarchy would ever allow. But more often than not, perhaps out of a sense of moral obligation, they provide the services for which they were originally employed for sufficiently lengthy periods.

'But what about pay?' Costa was impressed but still incredulous. 'Surely someone must decide who gets what?'

'No, no hierarchy is involved in determining pay either,' came Kosti's answer. A company's income is divided into five slices. One slice, 5 per cent of all revenues to be precise, is retained by the government. The remaining 95 per cent is divided into four: an amount to cover the firm's fixed costs (such as equipment, licences, utility bills, rent and interest payments), an amount for R & D, a slice from which basic payments to staff are made and, lastly, a slice for bonuses.

The relative size of those four slices is decided collectively on a one-person-one-vote basis. Anyone who wishes to propose a change in the current distribution has to put forward their new formula. For example, if they want an increase in the amount allocated to basic pay, they will need to say which other slice or slices will see the necessary reduction. If only a single alternative proposal for the following year's distribution is put forward, a simple two-way referendum suffices. More often than not, though, many competing business plans are put forward, each accompanied by an intricate rationale. Here a more complicated voting system is used.

Before voting, staff are given at least a month to read up on each proposal, to debate them and to form their preferences. They are then invited to rank the proposals in order of preference on an electronic ballot form. If no plan wins an absolute majority of first preferences, a process of elimination takes place. The plan with the fewest first preferences is knocked out and its first-preference votes are reallocated to the voters' second preferences. This simple algorithmic process is repeated until a plan has acquired more than half the votes cast.

Having determined the amounts of money the company will spend on the various slices, the basic pay slice is then divided equally among all staff – from those recently employed as secretaries to the firm's star designers or engineers.

Costa appreciated the simplicity of the system but could not see how the fifth slice, the bonuses, could be distributed democratically. 'Surely any decision as to who gets what bonus must involve a hierarchy?' he insisted.

'Do you recall the Eurovision Song Contest?' Kosti asked.

Costa did remember that hideous celebration of kitsch.

'Then you may recall the voting scheme at the end of all the awful singing: every participating country was given points to allocate to the songs of every other country, but not to its own song. The song that gained the most points won. We use essentially the same allocation system to determine the bonuses of each member of our corporation,' Kosti explained.

Every year, just before the New Year's holidays, Kosti is given one hundred merit points to distribute among his colleagues. He can give all his one hundred merit points to a single colleague whom he thinks has done a uniquely exceptional job or he can spread them out more thinly among colleagues whom he thinks have made above-average contributions to the company. Meanwhile, all his colleagues do the same, resulting in each member of the company receiving a percentage of the total merit points, and it is this which determines the percentage of the bonus fund they receive. If, for example, Kosti collects 3 per cent of the total merit points, his personal bonus will be 3 per cent of the firm's total bonus fund – whose size has already been determined via the preferential voting algorithm.

Perhaps because of his Mediterranean background, Costa's immediate concern was that such a system was open to abuse. 'If that were a Greek or Italian company,' he confided to Eva weeks later, 'I have no doubt that most people would seek reciprocal agreements with their friends and allies: "I'll award you my one hundred points if you return the favour."' But when he put this to Kosti, he received an interesting answer.

Actually, Kosti explained, this is not something that any one of his colleagues contemplates, but to help maintain the precious social norm, they rely on a special sort of artwork. In a large, dimly lit room, along with other artworks contributed by staff and friends, a laser-powered installation is kept on permanent display during the twelve months following the bonus allocation. This projects a hologram in which every member of staff is represented in the form of their chosen avatar. If they aren't immediately visible or recognizable, a simple interface can be used to identify and locate them. Between the avatars there are arrows of different thickness representing the flow of merit points between colleagues, with the thickness of the arrow in proportion to the number of merit points awarded. Any suspicious reciprocity is thus immediately apparent: when the thickest of arrows leaves Dave's avatar heading towards Tammy's, while Tammy's equally thick arrow goes in precisely the opposite direction, Dave and Tammy will have a hell of a job in the tea room explaining to colleagues this remarkable coincidence of mutual appreciation.

Costa was captivated. The corporation Kosti described had eliminated not only bosses and hierarchies but one of the crucial injustices of capitalism: that the owners of a company control its profits while those who work within it receive only a wage. The realization dawned on Costa that this was a company he would love to work for.

One person, one share, one vote

'None of us are free if one of us is chained.' Costa often found himself humming this rhythm-and-blues song, which reminds us that individual freedom is impossible unless slavery is eradicated wholesale and in all its forms. And he knew that the worst form of slavery is that which people consent to for lack of any viable alternative.

One summer in the early 1990s Costa had been holidaying in Thailand when he learned of a jeans factory nearby that had burned down in the middle of the night, incinerating almost the whole night shift. The reason so many died was that, to save money on security, management locked the building while the workers within toiled. To his horror, Costa learned that the workers had all signed forms giving their consent to this practice.

This extreme incident reinforced Costa's opinion that waged labour was a form of submission. Just as the ownership of one person by another is intolerable, irrespective of how well the master treats the slave, so too is an illiberal and unjust wage contract, whatever the wage or the working conditions. Unable to imagine how the masses could be liberated from the wage system, Costa focused his efforts on freeing himself – on becoming his own boss. The price he paid for this liberation – which he achieved by shorting shares and derivatives in the 2001 and 2008 stock exchange routs – was the partial sullying of his soul and, feeling like a fraud, he kept quiet about what he had done. But on the frequent occasions he found himself humming his own version of the song – 'If one of us is waged, none of us are free' – a pang from his guilty conscience made itself known.

And yet, what could he say to someone like Eva who would lose no time pointing out the impossibility of running an advanced industrial society without a system of waged labour? Supporting its elimination as a way to abolish unfair wages would make her laugh. The only thing Eva recognized as unfair was telling consenting adults they were not allowed to transact with one another on whatever terms they chose. Constraining that freedom was both unjust and stupid, as it would destroy the entrepreneurial drive that liberates us all from poverty and need.

Despite not having all the arguments sorted out in his head, Kosti's description of corporate life in the Other Now changed everything for Costa. He was now able to imagine a modern, high-tech corporation where everyone shared the firm's net revenues, albeit in proportion to the average opinion of their contribution, with no distinction between those who collected the profits and those who were paid a wage.

The elimination of bosses and hierarchies was no less significant. As a teenager in the mid-1970s, Costa had a school friend, Gregory, who was an anarchist. While most other teenagers, especially in Crete, were drawn to the Left and its anti-capitalist rhetoric, Gregory rejected it. Gregory was obsessed instead with the anarcho-syndicalist movement of the early twentieth century, especially the variety that arose around 1910 in Catalonia. Its central tenet was that power is civilization's worst enemy, especially when channelled through hierarchies, which only bring out the worst in us. Like left-wing radicals, anarcho-syndicalists opposed private rights over property and the noxious division of earnings between wages for minions and profits for the masters. But anarcho-syndicalists went a step further and opposed the state itself, which they saw as the main defender of those property rights and corporate hierarchies.

To avoid the tyranny of power, the anarcho-syndicalists that had shaped Gregory's thinking were committed to replacing corporate hierarchies with decentralized systems relying on equal rights and the principle of one person one vote. Their movement was, of course, thwarted by the antipathy of both the establishment and the communist left, as well as by the primitive technologies of the time, which impeded their ideas' implementation. But the ideas Gregory shared with Costa left a profound impression on him.

'Besides capital,' Gregory warned Costa, 'we must beware power.' It was a thought whose influence on Costa grew with time.

In the mid-80s, as part of his quest for alternatives to capitalism, Costa had taken a close look at the Soviet model of corporate management and economic planning. It left him distinctly cold. In theory Soviet companies were commonly owned and all their employees ostensibly shared the net revenues. And yet they were managed by hierarchies every bit as ruthless in their imposition of power relations as anything Henry Ford or Jeff Bezos ever concocted.

If Costa had learned anything from his experience of corporate life, it was that power perverts and hierarchies are effective only at reproducing themselves, begetting even more corrupting power. In fact, the formal ownership of a company is of less importance, he decided, than the way in which power is structured and reproduced within it. Even though the absence of private property rights limited the capacity of Soviet bosses to profit, it did not limit their hierarchies' dictatorial power over the workers, and often over consumers and local communities as well. So when in 1991 the communist system collapsed, Costa was saddened that the only alternative to capitalism that actually existed had disappeared, but he was not at all surprised. Gregory's warnings had prepared him to expect the Soviet Union's hierarchies to turn it from despotic collectivism into a system of industrial feudalism.

In one of his dispatches, Kosti asked Costa if he was still in touch with Gregory. 'He deserves to know that somewhere out there a new corporate reality is brimming with his ideas,' Kosti said.

How Costa would have loved to convey to Gregory the excellent news from the Other Now, but neither of them could track him down. In imagining Gregory's response, however, Costa realized he lacked answers to many of the harder questions he would have asked him. What kind of ownership structure supported the one-person-one-vote system of corporate decision-making? Who if anyone actually owned the company's capital, not just its financial reserves but also its good name, the capacity of its brand to stir something in people's hearts or minds? What happened when people fell out or wanted to leave?

Kosti's brief but arresting answers continued to arrive. No one could own shares in the company unless they worked in it, following a successful interview and an all-member vote admitting them. Those admitted were granted precisely one share. The fact that some members were regarded with greater esteem than others and were paid more, via higher bonuses, did not translate into more votes. They may have had more influence in the debates preceding any vote, just as a skilled orator in a parliament does, but the one-person-one-share-one-vote rule was paramount.

Gradually it dawned upon Costa that, as this company structure spread through the economy, outcompeting and replacing others, stock exchanges would have disappeared. Kosti confirmed that, by the early 2020s, stock exchanges had indeed shrunk into economic insignificance, resembling our markets for stamps or cryptocurrencies: present but inconsequential. Instead of the liquid, instantly tradable shares of Our Now, which grant their owners a claim over future profits produced by others, in the Other Now shares were similar to franchises: an automatic, non-transferable, personal right to participate on equal terms in the decision-making of the company one worked for.

The implication of this was momentous: for the first time since the inception of capitalism, the political and economic spheres had been reintegrated. Before capitalism, political and economic power had been indistinguishable. Princes were rich and only the rich were princes. Political power translated automatically into the power to extract wealth from others, through coercion or conquest. And the power to coerce translated into titles, castles, sceptres and tiaras. It was capitalism that had changed all this. With the establishment of international trading routes came the rise of merchants as a new class: economically powerful, despite their lack of political clout and lowly social standing. For the first time, economic power was distinct from political authority. The divorce was finalized when the merchants evolved into the major share-owners of industry and, eventually, global finance and technology. Iris had instilled these notions in Costa over the course of many long discussions.

In this context, one person one share one vote was truly revolutionary – a major step towards reintegrating the political and economic spheres. In our reality, we are accustomed to wielding power in political elections on the basis of one person one vote, but in shareholders' meetings one has as many votes as one has shares. The richer you are the more shares you can afford to buy and the more votes you can cast in favour of your own interests. This leads generally speaking to corporate strategies that maximize the dividends of the people or institutions hoarding the most shares, usually resulting in short-term gains for them at the expense of society's – and sometimes even the company's – long-term interests. And so the few with the many shares are able to accumulate even more shares, giving them more power to accumulate more shares, and so on indefinitely.

In contrast, Kosti and his colleagues can only ever own a single share each, which grants them a single vote and no more, to be cast in the all-member ballots that decide every corporate matter of strategic importance – from management and planning issues to the distribution of net revenues. Not only does this guarantee drastically lower income inequality, equal power encourages decision-making that favours collective, long-term interests rather than individual, short-term gain. And since spending in the marketplace is also a form of voting – when we choose to buy one brand of yoghurt over another, we lend some of our economic power to that yoghurt maker over its competitor – the lower income inequality of the Other Now promises a more equal say on what products society devotes its limited resources to producing.

To Costa, the benefits of such a system were immediately apparent, but what wasn't clear was how one could ever amass the means required to start a company in the first place. Costa was used to a world in which the stock market could fund a start-up – indeed, could make its owners stinking rich – years before the company made a single dollar of profit. 'Without a stock market,' Costa asked Kosti, 'how is capital formed and accumulated?'

Accumulation: democratized inequality

Kosti's answer was as follows. Every resident is provided with a bank account by the central bank. It is called Personal Capital or PerCap for short. Every person's PerCap comprises three funds that are kept separate by Chinese walls: Accumulation, Legacy and Dividend.

Kosti's income from business activity – basic pay and bonuses alike – is credited into his Accumulation fund within his PerCap. So, people working in companies that are doing better have higher Accumulation deposits, as do those who receive higher bonuses. In this sense, Accumulation is the least novel of the three PerCap funds and the realm in which inequality manifests itself freely. 'But do note that we are talking about a fully democratic inequality,' Kosti was keen to point out, 'in the sense that those receiving high bonuses do so not because of accumulated power, but because their colleagues used their one share one vote to grant them these payments on perceived merit.'

Legacy: a trust fund for every baby

All babies are born naked. Soon afterwards, however, some are dressed in expensive clothes and put on a path to a privileged life while the majority wear rags and must perform miracles to escape from a life of exhaustion, exploitation, servitude and fear. This is the kind of inequality that defines Our Now, from cradle to grave.

Not so in the Other Now. There, the moment a baby is born the state creates for it at the central bank a dedicated PerCap Legacy fund and credits that fund with a considerable sum of money, the same for all babies. Babies are still born naked but every one of them comes into the world with a bundle of capital provided by society.

This means that when they come of age and are ready to enter an existing business, or start one alone or with others, every youngster has some capital to deploy. To protect them from eating into it injudiciously, Legacy is the most illiquid of the three PerCap funds, with various hoops to be jumped through before anyone younger than sixty-five can tap into it.

Sure enough, some babies are born into privileged families, just as in Our Now. However, in the Other Now none are born into the hideous freedom Costa first read about as a child on the tombstone of his favourite author, Nikos Kazantzakis: I HOPE FOR NOTHING. I FEAR NOTHING. I AM FREE.

'But what happens to poor kids until they are old enough to tap into their Legacy?' asked Costa.

Dividend: a universal right to the proceeds of society's capital

Kosti explained that this is where the third fund within PerCap comes into play – Dividend. Into this the central bank deposits a monthly sum, the size of which is determined by one's age. Dividend is largely funded by corporate revenues received by the state. In effect, the state taxes all corporations, usually at 5 per cent of gross revenues, to provide a social payment to all its citizens. Together with Legacy, the trust fund a baby receives at birth, Dividend guarantees freedom from need as the baby grows into a child, a young adult and a citizen.

The monthly payment's purpose is to liberate everyone from the fear of destitution but also from the demeaning and cruel means testing of the welfare state. It provides people who do not care to engage in business activity with sufficient income to provide priceless contributions to society that no market can properly value – for example in the caring sector, environmental conservation or non-commercial art. 'To exercise their right to laziness even,' Kosti added provocatively.

Of all of Dividend's benefits, Kosti made a point of extolling one in particular: it liberates the poor from the so-called safety net that in fact entangles them in permanent poverty. Instead of a net that traps them, Dividend acts as a solid platform on which the poorer and the unluckier can stand, allowing them to reach for something better. It gives young people the freedom to experiment with different careers and to study non-lucrative topics, from Sumerian pottery to astrophysics. It single-handedly makes impossible the type of exploitation that, in Our Now, we take for granted in the so-called gig economy with its archipelago of zero-hours contracts.

Costa was aware of various proposals for different versions of universal basic income, many of which had been floating around since the 1970s. He had not liked them much. Like many left-wingers, he considered the right to laziness an essentially bourgeois concept. But his greatest qualm, as he explained to Kosti, was that using the taxes of a hard-working proletarian to pay for some bum to lounge around all day watching telly would only lead to division. 'It is antithetical to working-class solidarity,' he said.

'But you are forgetting that no one pays income or consumption taxes here,' replied Kosti. 'Dividend is a *return* to every citizen for their partial *ownership* of society's capital.'

Costa admitted he had not thought of that. Indeed, his appreciation of Dividend dramatically increased when Kosti pointed out that only two taxes were levied in the Other Now: corporate tax and land tax. No income tax. No sales tax or VAT. No one paid a penny to the state on their income or whenever they purchased something, a good or a service. Costa found it as difficult to get his head round this as Eva would later have accepting a society without a stock market. But once he had, he saw that Dividend made sense in a way that universal basic income had not in the 1970s and 1980s. The key was that Dividend was not financed by taxation; it was, rather, a real dividend that people received as co-owners of the capital stock they were collectively producing – even if they did not do what we readily recognize as work.

Wealth is like a language

One of Ludwig Wittgenstein's stunning observations was that no private language is possible. By definition, language is something that can only be produced collectively. Iris enjoyed pointing out that the same is true of wealth. In direct contradiction of the myth promoted by capitalists and rentiers that wealth is produced by individuals, only to be collectivized by the state through taxation, the reality, Iris argued, is that wealth, like language, can only be produced collectively. Only then is it privatized by those with the power to do so.

To illustrate her argument, she would point out that pre-modern forms of capital such as farmland and seeds were collectively developed through generations of peasant endeavour before being appropriated by landlords. Today, every Apple, Samsung, Google or Microsoft device relies on infrastructure and components that were originally developed thanks to a government grant or made possible by drawing on the commons of ideas that grew in the same way folk tales and songs do: communally. While big tech has eagerly appropriated all this socially produced capital – and made a mint in the process – it has never paid any dividends to society. And it does not stop there. Every time we search for something on Google, navigate using an app or post a photo on Facebook or Instagram, we add to those corporations' capital stock with our data. Guess who is collecting all the dividends?

Costa had long believed that the solution to this problem was higher taxation of big tech's profits or, in his more radical moments, the nationalization of Google and its ilk. Now he came to think that this Dividend that Kosti was describing was a far better scheme than either taxation or nationalization: that everyone is granted a right to share in the returns to capital stock merely reflects the collective investment on which corporations' capital relies. And because it is impossible to calculate the precise amount of social capital that any firm owes society in this way, the only way to decide what percentage of their revenues should be returned to society is by means of a democratic decision – namely, the legal stipulation that a slice of all corporate revenues (5 per cent in the case of Kosti's firm) should flow automatically into the central bank, from where it continues to flow so as to fund, in part, every baby's Legacy and every adult's Dividend. Just as Kosti and his colleagues share equally a slice of the corporation's revenues in the form of basic pay, so society shares equally a slice of the corporation's returns on capital in the form of basic income.

What a marvellous idea! Costa thought, his instinctive scepticism by now almost wholly swept away. And yet questions remained. In the absence of the investment and start-up capital provided by stocks and shares, how were corporations such as Kosti's ever formed? And what if Kosti were to fall out with his colleagues or wished to move on? Would he leave empty-handed?

Plain vanilla loans

Enterprises need people and resources. The recruitment of people in the Other Now did not strike Costa as being so radically different from what he was familiar with, notwithstanding the spontaneous and democratic nature of the hiring process. But when it came to the allocation of resources, the difference was truly radical.

Before private wealth emancipated him from the labour market, every job offer Costa had ever received came with thinly veiled encouragements to demonstrate his trust in the company by buying shares in it. Later on, he was offered share options: the legal, but rescindable, right to buy shares in the company on some future date at a fixed, low price. Share options are a powerful instrument in Our Now. They enrich insiders but are also a mighty disciplinary device – a juicy carrot dangled in front of you that can be removed at the drop of hat by your boss. By contrast, on the day of his appointment, Kosti was automatically handed his single share of the company he joined – for free, no strings attached, just as a student gets her library card or a new employee his security badge. The prospect of buying a few more shares in the company could not even have occurred to Kosti. Indeed, the success of the one-share-one-person system was that the very idea of buying and selling shares had become as appalling as the notion of a trade in votes or babies.

And yet a market for shares allows for savings – whether from an individual's bank account or from a large pension fund – to be put back into use as investment, the crucial mechanism on which companies in Our Now rely in order to be born and to grow. So how were people's savings put to work in the absence of such a market? How did companies raise funding? How did stored cash turn into actual investment? How did past labour's energy crystallize into new machinery, new means of producing stuff?

'Through direct lending to business facilitated by every person's PerCap account,' Kosti explained.

Upon being hired, Kosti was offered the chance to divert part of his PerCap holdings to the company. So, while he cannot buy ownership rights in corporations, he is allowed and encouraged to lend to them – especially to the corporation that he works for. The incentive to lend to one's new work community is twofold: a sense of reciprocal commitment and, more practically, the thought that otherwise the company will have to rely on loans from strangers, perhaps at a premium reflecting a higher risk assessment by outsiders. Of course, youngsters getting their first job have no savings stored in their PerCap's Accumulation, but if they wish they can lend their new company part of their PerCap Legacy – making first use of the trust fund society set up for them at birth.

But anyone is also at liberty to lend to a company other than their employer. And this is what Kosti had done. Over the years, he had lived off his company basic pay and the monthly Dividend, saving his bonuses into his Accumulation, from which he then lent to other companies whose wares and services to the broader community he felt should be supported, accruing interest on the monies he had lent. Were he to move on to another corporation, Kosti would take with him his PerCap, from which he might choose to lend to his new company. A free market for plain vanilla savings thus ensures that businesses have access to people's PerCap and, in turn, savers have access to a liquid market that makes good use of their PerCap savings.

As for what happens when a member of staff leaves a company, it's simple: one ups stumps and goes one's way with whatever one's PerCap contains. Dismissals are, naturally, more painful. In the same way that anyone within the company can invite others to help set up a search committee to recruit new staff, they can also set up a board of inquiry into whether it is time to let go an underperforming or misbehaving colleague. Once the committee has heard from all sides and deliberated in full view of any staff wishing to observe the distressing proceedings, an all-member vote decides the matter.

The PerCap account that everyone owns from birth makes all this much easier. Whether joining or leaving corporations, it follows you wherever you go. Whether Kosti leaves his firm voluntarily or is fired, no golden handshake or compensation is legally required. Of course, if his colleagues wish to, they can vote to transfer part of their pay, basic or bonus, to him as a gift in acknowledgement of the service he has contributed to the enterprise, or as a means of soothing a dismissal's unpleasantness. Otherwise, Kosti will exit carrying with him only his PerCap.

In the limited space Kosti had to explain the Other Now's corporate law, he added two important details. The first one concerned the arrangements for dissolving small corporations or partnerships. When two colleagues no longer see eye to eye, the impossibility of a majority vote prevents a decision on who keeps the company and who departs. In such cases, the Shootout Clause is activated: each submits a sealed number representing the financial value they assign to staying on. When the numbers are revealed, the higher bidder keeps the company. However, the price of keeping it is that she or he will have to lend the company, from her or his PerCap, a sum equal to the winning bid – and also pay a state tax proportional to the bid. The Shootout's design means that the partner who thinks more highly of the company's capacity to repay its debt, and contribute to society, gets to keep it.

The second detail answered another concern of Costa's: how are corporations made to take into account the interests of those who don't work directly for them – of consumers, communities and society at large?

Socialworthiness

In Our (capitalist) Now, the only interests that company directors are legally obliged to serve are those of their shareholders. The rest of us must live in hope that the state and its agencies are not 'captured' by big business but will protect us against it, at least to some extent.

Yet, over the past two centuries, the cartel of mega-firms and mega-banks running the world have proved adept at watering down, bypassing and ultimately making a mockery of the regulatory frameworks designed to constrain them: from banking rules and labour protections to environmental standards and local community consultations. In Costa's view, the rise of big tech had made a bad situation markedly worse, with Facebook and its ilk turning abuse of their users into an Olympic sport. What would Costa not give to witness their neutering?

In the Other Now, Kosti explained, corporations are by nature much less commanding. The lack of stock exchanges and companies' flat management structures keep their size relatively small – typically, no more than a few hundred staff. Nevertheless, Kosti was keen to point out that the public had demanded mechanisms that guaranteed corporate accountability to society. Hence the Other Now's Social Accountability Act, which stipulates that every corporation is graded according to a Socialworthiness Index by regional panels of randomly selected local citizens known as Citizens' Juries. These representative panels are drawn not from the entire pool of the general public, however, but from a digital stakeholder community, formed whenever a new company is registered, which can be joined at any time by its customers, users and the communities served or affected by it. Every company's conduct, activities and effects on communities is eventually monitored by these juries, who periodically grade the company using a standardized social ratings system, developed and refined over time across different industries and jurisdictions. Once checked and settled, these ratings are published online, available at the touch of a screen to anyone.

The juries' social ratings are designed to encourage those within a company to care about those outside it. If a company's ratings fall consistently below a certain threshold, a public inquiry is ordered that may result in the company's deregistration – in which case the firm will either be shut down or put out to tender, so that any other group interested in trying to run it better has the opportunity to do so. Though this happens infrequently, the very existence of this Damoclean sword is what curbs exploitative practices. However, Citizens' Juries' social ratings make their most significant difference at another, subtler level.

It is human nature to bask in the glory of, or to recoil ashamed from, the organization one is, or was, part of. Eva, for example, was stigmatized by her Lehman past, which depleted much of the social capital she had gained at Stanford. The moment Lehman's shares tanked, she rapidly transitioned from master of the universe to pariah. It is also humanity's natural, though admittedly disagreeable, tendency to want to quantify and rank one another using numbers. But whereas in Our Now, there is only one, albeit constantly fluctuating, number with which to do so – a company's share price – in the Other Now share prices do not exist and the juries' social ratings fill the void.

Kosti reported that his company's social ratings rubbed off on him. In professional contexts, people tend to check on one another's company ratings before embarking on a collaboration or negotiations for a deal. Inevitably these social ratings spill over into the personal sphere and are used more casually, in the same way one looks online at customer reviews of a product or a film.

Perhaps most importantly, if Kosti wanted to move on and apply for a job at a new company, those taking an interest in him would scrutinize not only his personal record but also his company's social standing. Naturally, their first port of call would be Kosti's personal record, reflected in the voting record of his colleagues – the merit points they granted him over the years when allocating bonuses. But hiring committees would also scrutinize the collective appreciation or otherwise of his company within the broader community – just as students in Our Now look at the league tables for universities when evaluating a particular course.

Costa could see the attraction. But he was also struggling to fend off a sense of repugnance. Turning people into numbers was awful, he felt. The surest way to destroy a quality is to turn it into a quantity. Was this not what capitalism had done to us? Reduce every value to a price, every exchange into a transaction, every thing of incalculable beauty into a measurable object of desire? And yet, despite his idealism, Costa also recognized that a democratic, technologically advanced, large-scale economy cannot be run like a commune. It needs numbers. Quantification is unavoidable.

'If we are to be turned into numbers, we might as well design a system in which the numbers are determined democratically,' he opined.

'Randomness is the great ally against tyranny,' Kosti replied. 'If the juries determining our numbers were chosen by any other process than purely random selection, they would be open to influence and ultimately exploitation and tyranny. Even if they were determined by elections, for example, then a new oligarchy would soon be created. We borrowed this fabulous idea from the ancient Athenians, in fact. However sexist and imperialistic ancient Athenians were, it was remarkable that almost all the city's officeholders, including its judges, were randomly selected. They loathed elections – and were on to something!'

Reflecting on all that Kosti had described, Costa looked out of the window of his laboratory. He saw San Fransciscans going about their business and realized that each of them was carrying around their necks the invisible albatross of a number – a number that, for most people, was steeped in pain, resulting in sleepless nights over unpaid bills and mortgages. A number calculated opaquely by the same people that helped cause the 2008 crash by giving their hearty approval to the bankers' most appalling practices. A number that widens the gulf between private wealth and poverty, that reflects a person's power in a society that has abolished any prospect of economic democracy. A repulsive number mirroring a repulsive system. That number was their creditworthiness score.

'If we are to carry around a number,' Costa acknowledged, 'it might as well convey our socialworthiness, not our creditworthiness. A number that is produced transparently, collectively and by randomly chosen fellow citizens – not by the bankers' handmaidens.'

TATIANA lives!

Every piece of information he gathered about the Other Now made Costa think of Iris. What would she be thinking? He tried to imagine the questions she would put to Kosti. And he feared her ire if she were to find out that he had so far learned nothing about the Other Now's handling of issues like patriarchy, racism, sexual politics, democracy, climate change. He surprised himself by also thinking that Eva would have worthy questions to add about aspects of Kosti's world, particularly the extent to which personal liberty was safeguarded there.

Caught up in the excitement, he had not contacted Iris since 7 April, the day he ran that fateful test on Cerberus. As for Eva, though they had hardly seen each other for years, Iris had somehow managed to keep her in his mind through frequent mentions of their most noteworthy quarrels. Now that he held the key to the Other Now, these two people, in their very different ways, were uniquely placed to help him make sense of it. Time to take a break from HALPEVAM and pay them a visit.

Before travelling to Brighton, he needed to give Iris some notice. An enigmatic message only she could decrypt would do nicely, especially if it promised to dispel one of her primal fears: that Thatcher might have been right. That maybe financialized capitalism was, warts and all, better than the feasible alternatives. That perhaps, in the absence of fathomable alternatives, our commodified present was our only viable option.

Back in the 1980s, Iris had railed at public meetings against Thatcher's famous claim, 'There Is No Alternative', referred to as TINA, and in favour of TATIANA, her radical, Thatcher-busting cousin – the opposing doctrine That Astonishingly There Is AN Alternative. After almost two months of messaging with Kosti, Costa sent Iris the triumphant message: 'TINA was a lie. TATIANA lives. I have the proof. See you next week.'

A week later, he set off for Brighton to explain in person.

4

How Capitalism Died

The end of banking

Costa had no idea how he could persuade Iris and Eva to take him seriously. Convincing them that the Other Now existed and that he had found a way to communicate with the Other Costa seemed unlikely. And yet his real fear was what might happen if he succeeded.

He was certain Iris would take him to task for having put to Kosti all the wrong questions. And he expected Eva to complain that his questions did not address money, the role of government and, above all else, property rights over land and scarce resources. His planned defence was to invite them to think of this first set of transcripts as an appetizer – and of his visit's purpose as their opportunity to contribute questions that he would then put to Kosti.

Throughout the long-haul flight to Gatwick and the taxi ride from there to Iris's home, Costa's mind was racing. Besides fretting over Iris and Eva's unpredictable reactions to his inconceivable news, something else was nagging at him. In his guts he knew he had missed something big, that he had failed fully to grasp the import of Kosti's dispatches. Shortly before touchdown, a massive realization hit him: *These bastards have eliminated the banks!*

There could be no doubt. Kosti had said that everyone kept, from birth, a digital account with the central bank – their

PerCap. Each PerCap comprised Legacy, socially inherited capital holdings; Dividend, essentially an account where the state deposited a monthly amount; and Accumulation, a savings account where all other incomes ended up. Assuming that everyone can make any kind of payment they need to out of this one account, why would they ever need a commercial bank account as well? The whole purpose of retail commercial banks had disappeared.

And so too for the investment banks. It often struck Costa how few people really understood what they do. Despite their name, one thing they do not do is invest – at least, not in skills, equipment, solar panels, hospitals or anything else of tangible value. Investment bankers spend their considerable energies and talents conjuring up complicated trades involving debt and shares. First they create fiendishly complicated forms of debt, exactly as Eva had done at Lehman. Then they sell these so-called debt instruments to speculators such as large pension funds looking for a return on the accumulated contributions of their employees, who bet that these debt instruments will increase in price. Investment bankers then lend all the money they have amassed in return for these debt instruments to their clients, who in turn use it to invest heavily in selected shares, thereby turbocharging their price. The higher they drive these share prices, the more customers the investment banks find to buy their ever-more-complicated bundles of debt and shares. This mutual reinforcement of debt and share prices is a closed circle, and so the world of money is decoupled from the real world, in which most people struggle, and leads eventually to a handful of super-funds owning almost everything.

But take tradable shares out of the equation and the whole structure evaporates. Costa now realized that the only remaining purpose of investment banks was to help people lend their money to corporations like Kosti's. And while such brokers exist in the Other Now, plain vanilla lending reduces their power to almost zero. Kosti and everyone else have access to the same digital central bank payment system and are at liberty to lend simply and transparently to anyone within it using one of many competing apps playing the role of intermediary. No room is left for any financier to act as superpowerful go-between.

It had always struck Costa as the most extraordinary racket how in Our Now the banks and their most powerful clients create power for each other out of thin air. First the bankers grant their rich customers outsized overdraft facilities with which to buy shares. Thus, entirely fictitious money is used to acquire bits of different companies. Then, rather than treating those shares as investments, the bankers' preferred clients don't hang around waiting for the companies to make a profit and pay a dividend. Instead, they simply sell their shares on at a higher price. To whom? To other money men who also use fictitious money provided by some other bank overdraft.

As long as this racket continues, the trade in shares roars and their price soars. If the companies do happen to make a profit, share prices soar even higher. As share prices rise, the money men ratchet up immense paper profits, leaving bankers with a juicy cut. And when the bubble bursts, and the overdrafts turn into black holes in the banks' books, the bankers dial the number of their favourite politician, whose campaign they featherbedded, and, before anyone notices, their losses are transferred to the taxpayers – many of whom the banks evict from their homes after foreclosing on their mortgages. *No wonder our financiers think of themselves as masters of the universe*, thought Costa. Almost totally disconnected from actual profits, capitalism is powered by fictitious capital flowing from convoluted trades in profits that have not yet materialized – and may never do so!

'Who needs mythology when reality is so unreal?' Costa had once wondered, when discussing this with Iris.

'We all do. Never underestimate the human need for soothing lies,' had been her reply.

He could hardly disagree, and yet it bewildered him that people truly believed capitalism to be about making things or providing services at a profit. He found it extraordinary how most people disliked speculators but thought of them as peripheral, as harmless bubbles on a steady stream of enterprise.

'They fail to recognize that the very opposite is true!' he had said to Iris. 'That enterprise long ago became a bubble on a whirlpool of speculation. That, in reality, workers, inventors and managers resemble driftwood buffeted hither and thither on a manic torrent of runaway finance. No one I know gets it: real power stems not from making real things but from this bizarre flux.'

As he came through passport control at Gatwick, the full significance of the abolition of tradable shares in the Other Now was making his head spin. It was, figuratively, the equivalent of damming the whirlpool of financial speculation until its torrent is reduced to a tepid stream – but a stream of real, not fictional, economic energy. In the wonderfully boring financial world of the Other Now, a Lehman Brothers, a JP Morgan or a Goldman Sachs could not exist.

As his taxi pulled over outside Iris's Brighton terrace, the butterflies in Costa's stomach were in a frenzy. Where does one start telling friends famous for their scepticism that another world, where capitalism had died, was not only possible but in fact already in existence? That TATIANA lived in the form of a society humming along without stock markets, bosses, means-tested benefits or banks? That, even though people were equally flawed and technologies were nowhere near as advanced as they appear on *Star Trek*, such a world was for real?

'They'll laugh in my face,' he said aloud without realizing it.

'Is everything OK, sir?' the taxi driver asked.

'Yes, yes. I'm fine,' he said irritably. 'For now.'

As soon as he alighted from the taxi, Eva emerged onto the street to greet him. And before he had a chance to knock on Iris's front door, she popped her head out of an upstairs window and said, 'Ah, you're here. Good.'

It would not be long before he would have to deliver the hardest presentation of his life to the toughest of audiences.

OC rebels

Even if Kosti's dispatches helped him convince Iris and Eva of the Other Now's plausibility, the main problem would be explaining how it had come about. One reason was Kosti's greater eagerness to describe how things worked in the present than to tell stories from the 'Three Years That Changed the World', as he referred to the period from 2008 to 2011. It left Costa with relatively little to go on. The best he could do with the fragments that Kosti had sent over was begin at the beginning: with the Occupy Movement that they all knew well.

In the Other Now, the Ossify Wall Street movement, as it was known, sprang up in New York City just as Occupy Wall Street had in Our Now. However, over there it went global under the name Ossify Capitalism, or OC for short. At the time Costa had been excited by Occupy Wall Street and its various equivalents worldwide: the Indignados in Spain, who in their tens of thousands took over the *plazas* of the main Spanish cities; the Greek Aganaktismenoi, who made Syntagma Square their own for three joyous months in the spring of 2011; the Nuit debout gatherings a few years later in Paris. Alas, that early promise fizzled out as fast as it materialized – especially after the surrender of the Obama administration to Wall Street in early 2009 and of the Greek leftist government to the oligarchy-without-frontiers in the summer of 2015. The great difference between the two movements was that the OC rebels recognized the futility of occupying spaces – squares, streets or buildings.

'Capitalism does not live in space but in time and in the ebb and flow of financial transactions,' was how Esmeralda, one of its impromptu leaders, put it.

The team she led was known as the Crowdshorters. According to Kosti, it was the first group to demonstrate the vulnerability of financialized capitalism and the power of a well targeted digital rebellion. Its first success came when it took direct aim at the financial instruments of mass destruction that played such an important role in causing the 2008 global crash: collateralized debt obligations.

These CDOs were a form of synthetic debt with which Eva would have been intimately familiar, having played a part in their manufacture while at Lehman. They can be imagined as boxes in which their creator places many tiny chunks of debt: a few pounds of the mortgage owed by Jill to her local bank, a few yen owed by Toyota to a Japanese pension fund, a few euros owed by a Greek bank to a German one, a few dollars owed by the US Federal Government to JP Morgan, and so on. Each CDO was filled with countless chunks of different types of debt, each with its own risk of default and interest rate.

The great selling point of CDOs was the fiction that they were a safe bet. Since they contained so many different pieces of debt owed by such a diversity of people and organizations, buyers were told that there was no chance that more than a few of those chunks would turn sour at once. Moreover, each CDO was so complex it was impossible for any human, even its creator, to estimate its value, so there was no real limit to what it could sell for: those who created, sold and traded in CDOs simply let the market decide, and no one in the market could argue that they knew any better. They were an invention worthy of a Bond villain, the ideal snake oil: pieces of paper that were, at once, completely opaque and yet apparently safe and lucrative. The false sense of security they offered led to far higher demand – and far higher prices – than CDO creators expected. Observing bankers' surprise at the high prices, others flocked in to place their orders, boosting prices ever higher.

With so much money being made, the bankers who had created the CDOs soon forgot their original purpose: to offload bad debt onto gullible victims. Unable to stand by as others profited from their creations, bankers like Lehman lost their faculties and began to buy back their CDOs. The more they bought, the higher the already stratospheric prices went, the greater the paper value of their stacks of CDOs, and the larger their bonuses. Delirious with their profits, the bankers borrowed mountains of money from each other to buy even more CDOs.

In short, the bankers fell headlong into their own trap. And when all of the bad debts inside those CDOs turned sour and the bottom fell out of the market in 2008, the financiers fell into a bottomless pit of their own making. As they sank, the politicians and the major central banks – the Fed, the Bank of England, the ECB and all the rest – rushed in to re-float them. That's when Esmeralda's Crowdshorters struck.

Techno-rebels

Esmeralda, like Eva, had worked for one of the large financial houses until just before the crash, and thus understood their inner workings well. Using her expertise, her Crowdshorters undermined the central banks' efforts surgically and stylishly. They realized what few understood: by privatizing everything, capitalism had made itself supremely vulnerable to financial guerrilla attacks. Specifically, Esmeralda recognized that the creation of CDOs out of plain debt – a process known hubristically and ironically as securitization – afforded the perfect opportunity for a peaceful grassroots revolution.

The consequence of having privatized all the utility companies was that every telephone, water or electricity bill incurred by residents in Croydon or small businesses in Preston was owed to some private corporation. However, the corporation had pre-sold these payments ages before to some financier. What exactly had the financier bought? The right to collect the future revenue streams from the little people. And what did the financier do with that right? Sliced it up into tiny chunks and placed them in different CDOs, which in turn were sold on to other financiers – globally!

Esmeralda and her comrades had the technical skills to unpick the contents of every CDO. Painstakingly, they wrote software that could identify precisely which chunk of debt within each CDO was owed by which household, when each chunk of a bill or a debt repayment was due, to whom it was owed, and who owned the specific CDO at every point in time. Using this vast database of information, they were then able to contact households – most of which were outraged by the bankers' behaviour and the bailouts they were set to receive – and invite them to participate in low-cost, targeted, short-term payment strikes – or crowdshorting as Esmeralda called these campaigns.

The Crowdshorters' pitch to residents was simple. In fact, one of the first of them – a circular sent by Esmeralda to Yorkshire residents – is now commemorated in the Other Now on a plaque that adorns the Houses of Parliament in London:

HELP US BRING DOWN THOSE PROFITING FROM YOUR EXORBITANT WATER BILL WHILE YOU ARE STRUGGLING TO PUT FOOD ON THE TABLE. JUST DELAY PAYING YOUR WATER BILL FOR TWO MONTHS, AND DON'T WORRY ABOUT THE LATE PAYMENT FEE. WE ARE CROWDSOURCING FUNDS TO COMPENSATE YOU. UNITED WE STAND, DIVIDED WE FALL!

Similar plaques are on display in the entrance to the Capitol building in Washington DC, even the Greek parliament on Syntagma Square.

The uptake was breathtaking. People all over the UK, soon the world, began to take great pleasure in tracking, and heeding, the Crowdshorters' calls. Their meticulously coordinated payment strikes caused cascades of crashes in the CDO market which spilled over into the major stock exchanges. Within three weeks, the central banks realized it would be impossible to re-float the bankers' trillions of dollars' worth of securitized debt while, at the same time, the privatized utilities were going bust and demanding bailouts too.

Unable to convince Congress to pump the missing trillions into Wall Street for a second and then a third time in the space of a few months, the US Federal Government had to allow Goldman Sachs, JP Morgan and the other behemoths to be wound down. The repercussions were immense. Europe's banks, which were in a far worse state than America's, shut up shop too. The City of London was in meltdown. Governments were forced to nationalize the failing utilities. The Fed, the European Central Bank, the Bank of England, the Bank of Japan, even the People's Bank of China, had no alternative but to step into the void and provide citizens with bank accounts – the first stirrings of PerCap.

While they played a central role in sinking global finance, Esmeralda and her Crowdshorters could not have sparked the OC revolution on their own. Wrecking an already collapsing Wall Street was one thing; ossifying capitalism was quite another. This is where other techno-rebels came into the picture.

Recognizing pension funds as the largest shareholders in the great corporations, a band of radicalized traders working out of Mumbai's financial centre and calling themselves Solidarity Sourcing Proxies – Solsourcers for short – decided it was time to target globalization's most ludicrous racket. Drawing inspiration from the Crowdshorters, the Solsourcers invited people to nominate companies with the worst record of zero-hours contracts, low pay, carbon footprints, working conditions and the tendency to 'downsize' in order to boost their share prices. Millions of people from all over the world pitched in to name the worst offenders. Then the Solsourcers organized the mass withholding of pension contributions to the pension funds that owned shares in those companies. The mere rumour that the Solsourcers had targeted a particular pension fund turned out to be enough to send its shares crashing and to cause an exodus of worried investors from equity funds related to it. The Solsourcers eventually needed only to send to a pension fund a list of the companies it wanted it to divest from, and the fund would do so immediately, lest its incoming pension contributions dried up.

Realizing their power, the Solsourcers spread their wings globally and began to make more ambitious and highly sophisticated demands, not merely for divestment from unscrupulous employers and environment-destroying corporations, but for reforms to corporate law. Inspired by a flat management structure pioneered by a corporation based near Seattle, they managed to take the first steps towards prescribing by law the corporate model one person one share one vote.

By early 2010, the Solsourcers had been joined by another group of techno-rebels. Calling themselves Bladerunners in homage to Rick Deckard, the fictional character whose job in a famous 1982 sci-fi movie was to hunt down and kill androids, they thought of themselves as neo-Luddites, even choosing as their patron figure Lord Byron, the poet laureate of the original Luddite movement. The Bladerunners did not fear technology, though. They celebrated the Luddites as history's most misunderstood figures, whose vandalism of machines was a protest not against automation but against social arrangements that used technological innovation to deprive the majority of their dignity and life prospects. Indeed, the Bladerunners embraced digital platforms, even the rise of AI, but were adamant that such machines should be utilized in the cause of shared prosperity, not as instruments of neo-feudalism or of a class war by the few against the many.

The Bladerunners' first target was big tech: mega-corporations with monopoly power that rendered them so rich they required neither Wall Street nor pension funds for their capital. Akwesi, one of their early leaders, had worked for Microsoft in the 1990s. In early 2009 Akwesi proclaimed that Google had inadvertently invented a new human right: the right to freely available and instantly accessible information.

'The problem with inventing a human right,' Akwesi explained playfully to a director at Google, 'is that you lose the right to monopolize its provision and, most certainly, to profit from supplying it.'

The Bladerunners organized mass consumer strikes, targeting one big tech company at a time. Their first successful mobilization was aimed at Amazon. Akwesi issued a global call to boycott Amazon for a day in support of doubling hourly pay in its warehouses around the world. That Day of Inaction, as the Bladerunners called it, caused less than a 10 per cent drop in Amazon's usual revenues. But that was enough for Amazon immediately to concede a 50 per cent pay rise. Encouraged by their success, the Bladerunners embarked on many more campaigns of widening scope.

Rallying support via social media, the Bladerunners' Days of Inaction became worldwide events, enjoying mass participation, especially by the young, until they needed only to announce their next target for its share price to fall precipitously and for there to be relentless scrutiny of its directors and their practices online. When in early 2012 they brought down Facebook and gained legal recognition for an individual's property rights over their private data, the Bladerunners knew they had grown sufficiently powerful to make history and effect serious societal change.

At around the same time the Bladerunners teamed up with the Environs in order to hasten the demise of the fossil fuel industry. Together, they forced panicking governments to introduce stringent limits to pollutants, to reduce net-carbon targets to zero by 2025 and even to limit land-clearing and cement production. Some influential corporations recognized that these constraints presented them with opportunities to profit from clean energy, but the OC rebels made it a condition for not targeting them too that they would drop out of the stock markets and give a single, non-tradable share to each member of their staff, thus laying the foundations for the corporations' conversion to an anarcho-syndicalist model.

Within three years, the Crowdshorters, the Solsourcers, the Bladerunners and the Environs had formed a highly effective network of targeted activism that the oligarchy-without-frontiers could not withstand.

Kosti had referred to this network as techno-syndicalism – adapting a term coined in the mid-1960s by John Kenneth Galbraith, an eminent twentieth-century American economist who referred to capitalism's network of power, its agglomeration of mega-firms and mega-banks, as the Technostructure. At first this had surprised Costa. He had never met anyone else familiar with that term. And then he remembered that until 2008 he and Kosti had been the same person.

This proved to be a curse as well as a blessing. Costa wished he could converse directly with Esmeralda, Akwesi and the other key players of the OC movement, the pioneers who had miraculously pushed capitalism beyond breaking point while sketching out and implementing fabulously novel social and economic arrangements. How he would have loved to cross-examine them on all aspects of this tremendous transition! But of course Cerberus prevented him from communicating with anyone in the Other Now who did not share his DNA. Total reliance on Kosti limited not just the range of information available to him but also the quantity. After a while, Kosti had grown impatient at Costa's 'tiresome historical questions'.

'Tiresome?' Costa exclaimed. 'I'd say these people deserve great tomes to be written about them!'

But to Costa's great frustration, Kosti refused thereafter to answer his queries about the past with anything more than a few snippets, bombarding him instead with minutiae reflecting his own preoccupations. And yet, so far as Costa could tell from the little Kosti would write about them, these bands of technologically savvy rebels boasted a rare blend of genius, courage and moderation – virtues hitherto absent from any successful revolutionaries. Another group, the Flying Pickets, embodied an international solidarity not seen since the International Brigades flocked to Spain in 1936 in an ill-fated attempt to defend democracy from Franco's fascist hordes. They set themselves the noble task of stopping multinationals from shifting exploitative practices from countries where the OC movement was flourishing to countries and jurisdictions

where it was weaker. So if a multinational corporation tried
to squeeze its Nigerian workforce to compensate for some
compromise it had made with the OC movement in the
United States, the Flying Pickets would orchestrate industrial
action in the United States against the same company, while
also liaising with the Solsourcers and the Bladerunners to act
against its stocks, bonds and sales.

The Wikiblowers were a key rebel group. These
anarchistic geeks proved crucial in preventing the established
order from regrouping in order to strangle the OC rebellion.
Their vital insight was that the most important advantage
that governments and corporations held over the general
population and the rebels was their access to and control over
surveillance information. The only way to stop Big Brother
was to level the playing field: to create a digital eye and train it
upon him so that everyone could see what he was up to.

Their main weapon was a piece of software they called the
Panopticon Code. Created collaboratively using open-source
tools, it was a remarkably infectious computer virus that lay
dormant and wholly undetectable, allowing it silently to infect
every computer network on the planet. Once it had penetrated
all networked devices on earth, the Wikiblowers activated it.
The result was immediate and total informational transparency.
Everyone could see everything. Citizens had access to every
state secret. Workers could read the files their bosses had on
them. Anyone could tune into any CCTV camera installed
anywhere in the world, from one on a lamp post to a military
drone. For the first time, the poor and the weak had the same
access to information as the rich and the powerful, even the
NSA itself. Within minutes the world changed. Governments
and corporations were paralysed by the billions of eyes trained

on them. Many families were divided, as relatives discovered awful secrets about one another. Lifelong friendships were tested. But with the tumult came also tranquillity. An eerie calm descended as the world became glued to its screens not knowing where or what to look at next.

The OC rebels made sure to guide the world's attention towards the activity of those clinging to power at their expense. The unveiling of a plot by several governments to intervene militarily against the OC in several countries at once caused a global uproar. But gradually outrage at what was being revealed gave way to calls for reform: for democratization of the workplace, for an end to surveillance by the few, for demilitarization. The Wikiblowers had not merely prevented a coordinated and most likely lethal multi-state attack on techno-syndicalism's activists. No, they had accomplished something much grander: they had let the genie of people power out of the bottle. Once it had been set free, there was nothing the establishment could do to force it back in.

The final group Costa was able to learn anything about were the Infiltrators, whose task seemed to him the least fun. They began their campaigns by infiltrating existing political parties of every sort and in every country with a view to infecting them with the OC spirit. Wherever entryism did not work, the Infiltrators helped OC activists form new parties, movements and unions. Their overriding goal was the institution of participatory forms of democracy, such as those that ruled within Kosti's corporation and which could not have been sustained, Costa surmised, without a similar spirit energizing democracy regionally, nationally and transnationally.

Naturally, the OC rebellion manifested itself differently in different countries. Setbacks punctuated its progress, and in many cases the rebels had to compromise. Nevertheless, no country proved immune to the rebellion's transformative wave, just as the 1848 and 1991 revolutions had touched everyone, in one way or another, around the globe. Political institutions changed everywhere, even while they maintained many apparent features of the pre-existing ones. In the United States, for instance, radical transformation was portrayed as a natural evolution of the Founding Fathers' original intentions. Congress was forced to accommodate citizens' assemblies, as were the Houses of Parliament in the United Kingdom. In China, changes to corporate law were presented as the logical extension to Deng Xiaoping's break with Maoism in the 1990s. In continental Europe, they were introduced in new treaties helping to shore up the crumbling European Union. Ironically, it was in the countries that had emerged from the former Soviet Union, most notably Russia, that oligarchic capitalism proved most resilient.

'The strangest thing,' wrote Kosti, 'is that the traditional Left had very little to do with bringing down capitalism and instituting the economic democracy that we leftists dreamed of before anyone else dared to.' *This is the type of message Iris could warm to*, thought Costa.

Back to the fold

And so Costa now stood on Iris's doorstep, preparing to share this sensational story with the only people he could trust. Normally, the part of any get-together that he craved and feared in equal measure was the obligatory preliminaries: the hugs, the 'how have you beens', the cups of tea, the mandatory small talk. This time, it was their conclusion that he feared and craved most. Sure enough, after he had been ushered into Iris's kitchen, and Eva had joined them, and the greetings had been made, Iris's liberating question did not take long to come: 'So, what brings you here? Is it too much to hope that Tatiana is a girlfriend rather than an obsession?'

5

The Reckoning Begins

Suspending disbelief

Iris would have none of it. For almost two hours she mocked, teased and toyed with Costa, frustrating his efforts to describe what Kosti had revealed to him. And when he mentioned that he and Kosti shared identical pasts up until the autumn of 2008, her scorn got the better of her.

'How do we know that the timeline did not also split back in 1929?' she asked sarcastically. 'Or at the height of the Second World War? Or at the moment Hiroshima was obliterated? Or during the Vietnam War? Or on that day in 2020 when a mindless virus placed us all in lockdown for months on end? Or, indeed, every time Wolverhampton Wanderers score?'

'Maybe it did!' he replied. 'Maybe there are countless alternative realities to our own branching out every moment. It's the only plausible explanation. But so what? For whatever reason, I happen to have stumbled across this one. Maybe HALPEVAM led me to it, knowing it was closest to my heart. At any rate, the existence somewhere out there of other forks in the road, leading to an infinitude of different realities, is irrelevant – as irrelevant as all the other what-ifs you can think of but can never be tested. Kosti's dispatches are a golden opportunity. Surely we should grab it with both hands!'

Help came from an unexpected quarter. While Eva harboured the Panglossian belief that, however dissatisfied or unhappy we may be, we live in the best of all possible worlds, she was ready to engage in thought experiments with the impossible. And besides, despite her own incredulity, she was not going to miss out on an opportunity to show up Iris as stubborn and closed-minded.

'I don't mind assuming that your Kosti is alive, well and lives in a mythical Other Now,' she told Costa, visibly enjoying Iris's irritation. 'Accepting incredible assumptions can be a gateway to enlightenment. You may remember, Iris, how Descartes invented a non-existent and impossible number – the square root of minus one – in order to lampoon those prepared to accept any old rubbish as plausible, just as disrespectful atheists ridicule believers for keeping an imaginary bearded friend up in the sky. And yet, a century or so later, those mathematical geniuses Euler and Gauss showed how many crucial problems can be solved if we are prepared to suspend disbelief and assume that this imaginary number exists. Indeed, modern technology would be impossible without that little imaginary number. Come on, Iris, be a sport. Let's see where we end up if we assume that Kosti's world exists. Let's throw ourselves down Costa's rabbit hole.'

Iris was taken aback by Eva's open-mindedness.

'Delusions of scientific grandeur make you economists refreshingly open to mad assumptions,' she said. 'But never ones that put capitalism in question.' But grudgingly impressed by Eva's unexpected willingness to countenance Kosti's post-capitalist Other Now, she dropped her opposition to discussing the dispatches Costa had brought with him from San Francisco. Suddenly it was game on.

For six straight hours they pored over every paragraph that had made it through the wormhole. Months later, Iris would acknowledge that on that day – Thursday 12 June 2025 –the process of reading, debating and questioning Kosti's account brought the three of them closer to one another than they ever had been before. The process drew them into a shared mindset that it was impossible ever to leave or for anyone else to join. Piecing together and understanding the Other Now became an obsession well before Iris and Eva actually believed in its existence.

Why was this? What was it about the Other Now that brought them together in this way? A shared history of disillusionment, is my hypothesis: Eva's faith in benign, liberal capitalism, Iris's faith in revolutions to yield emancipation rather than horrors, Costa's faith that technology could democratize society – all had been shattered. In the face of their shared melancholy, Kosti's dispatches left open the possibility that their faith might not have been misplaced – that the world could be otherwise. The year 2008 was a poignant one for each of them. Studying Kosti's dispatches thus turned into a shared attempt to mend their broken dreams.

Eva approached the dispatches as she would an academic paper, treating Kosti's description of corporate life in the Other Now as Euler and Gauss had treated Descartes' imaginary number. Iris quickly became emotionally invested in the possibility of the radical alternatives that she had once lived for finally being realized. Costa, meanwhile, basked in the respite from his solitude.

Varieties of oppression

Iris did not buy it: having no boss sounded peachy but in reality she was sure it hid a multitude of sins, despite what Kosti claimed.

'Flat management does not automatically mean the end of oppressive hierarchies,' she said. 'Kosti's company could easily be a despotic workplace despite its lack of a formal power pyramid. After all, humans created ruthless patterns of oppression well before any law, civic or corporate, was written down.'

It was a lesson she had learned the hard way, she explained. As a young lecturer entering the self-proclaimed 'community of scholars' in the 1970s, male colleagues took it for granted that she would take the minutes or make the tea. It wasn't the law. It was something worse: a shared expectation that inhabited the common room just as patriarchy did the wider world.

It was a common mistake to think that laws and written rules create networks of power. No, power networks emerge first. They do so organically and only then crystallize into codes, rules, regulations and, finally, law. Removing the rules that enshrine hierarchy in law will not end hierarchy any more than the retreat of organized religion has eliminated superstition. Iris was not questioning that in Kosti's company everyone enjoyed formal self-management. 'But I bet some people are more self-managed than others.'

Her objection went deeper than doubting the flatness of the management system Kosti described. Experience with male-dominated power networks had led Iris to the conclusion that human nature hates a hierarchy vacuum and will find myriad ways to fill it with subtle forms of oppression and control. After all, it is in the egalitarian schoolyard that bullies are at liberty to build their sick little empires. Hierarchies protect the weak even while they oppress them; that is their quid pro quo. She had witnessed too many comrades commandeer democratic institutions, from trade unions and town hall meetings to cooperatives and neighbourhood action groups. It was the reason that she, a consummate syndicalist, had retreated into her tiny private sphere in Brighton – and the same reason led her to be instinctively suspicious of boss-less corporations.

'Given the choice between a formal oppressive hierarchy and an informal one,' she said, 'I think I probably prefer formalized oppression to hidden coercion presented as collegiality in action.'

Eva's objection to flat management was more prosaic.

'It sounds great' – she chuckled – 'until you try to get anything done without anybody telling anyone else what to do.'

Democratic partnerships, she argued, may work reasonably well for a while within a circle of well-mannered architects or solicitors – as long as the partners are not asked to accept the absurd idea that menial staff should be handed equal voting rights. But even then, Eva was adamant that such relationships never survive success or time: as partnerships grow, management by consensus becomes cumbersome. The inevitable inefficiency begets discontent. Retirements and new recruits constantly throw spanners in the works. Sooner or later the whining leads to breakdown. If flat management was a reliable model, Eva was convinced, it would have evolved in Our Now.

It was at this point that Costa, who until then had been relishing his silent role, spoke up. He reminded Eva that in Our Now, in the UK alone, at least twenty million people were working in the voluntary sector under managers with no right to fire them, force them to do things or even discipline them. And the outfits these volunteers staffed, which included lifeboat, firefighting and other essential social services, were remarkably efficient. Without such voluntary organizations, the 2020 epidemic would have claimed many more lives than it did. The question, as far as Costa was concerned, was whether the whole economy could emulate the voluntary sector.

Iris was shaking her head, not at Costa but at Eva, who was intentionally missing her point.

'It's not that democratic partnerships are inherently inefficient,' Iris said. 'As Costa points out, order can be generated spontaneously even if no boss is formally anointed. No, it's that democratic partnerships are too efficient at empowering the entitled while sneakily disempowering the rest of us.' A formal right to having no boss, when in reality you are being bossed around, may be worse than being subject to a boss whose powers are formally prescribed and thus contestable, she argued.

'As a liberal' – Iris addressed Eva directly – 'you must surely agree that the real question to be answered here is: how can power over persons be contained? How can bullies be kept in check in the workplace and beyond? Is flat management a good start in the fight against patriarchy?'

The evidence is mixed, Iris went on. On the one hand, the worst abuses take place in formally egalitarian spaces, the home being the most striking. On the other hand, as Costa had reminded them, millions of people demonstrate daily that it is perfectly possible for organizations to function well under consensual management.

'Don't you think you might be straining at a gnat and swallowing a camel?' Eva replied. For Eva, a far greater cause for concern – the camel in the room – was not the lack of hierarchy but the ban on trading company shares. Worrying about a bossy colleague having a little too much power, as Iris did, was a luxury compared to the gross threat to reason and liberty represented by the prohibition of selling shares in a business that one was trying to build up or get started. 'Stopping people from buying into a business is bad enough,' she said, 'but doing it in the name of democratizing power is to add insult to injury.'

Eva didn't know where Costa's dispatches actually came from but assumed that one way or another they were an expression of his own utopian fantasies. As such, she found it heartening that Costa did not envisage replacing free markets – which she had spent years defending to her lefty friends – with the usual collectivist nightmare. She was delighted, in fact, that Costa's utopia contained corporations in which staff were free to move about unimpeded by a nanny state. It was a marked improvement that Costa had graduated from total opposition to free-market capitalism to idealization of markets without capitalism. And yet, the more she thought about it the more she realized that Costa's rehashed socialism was perhaps even more of a threat to liberty and rationality than the old Stalinist project. Embracing markets but banning the market for shares was a brilliant move that Eva felt she had to counter with all her strength.

'The notion of stopping people from selling part of their business is the first step along the road to serfdom,' she said heatedly. 'It challenges the inalienable right of consenting adults to transact with each other. If Jill wants to sell an apple to Jack, or some portion of her business, and Jack agrees to buy it, what right has anyone to stop them?'

It was as if Eva had contrived to turn Iris from a sceptic into the Other Now's champion.

Liquid ownership

Is trading shares as simple and benign as Jill selling an apple to Jack? Is the ban on trading shares legislated, according to Kosti, in the Other Now, a violation of liberty and an act of folly? Or is it an excellent idea, the equivalent of a ban on selling votes in a democracy? That was the question, Iris and Eva agreed. What they disagreed on, naturally, was the answer.

Eva's answer required no complicated philosophical arguments or historical analysis. A share is simply a contract that entitles the purchaser to a slice of a company's future profits, she said. If there is nothing wrong with Jill selling Jack a number of apples, how can it possibly be wrong to sell him a share in the future harvest of her orchard? The only difference was that, in buying a portion of an apple harvest not yet produced, Jack was accepting a degree of risk. If, for example, a hail storm destroyed some of the apples before they were picked, he would end up with fewer of them. But if Jack is happy to pay his money despite the risk, who are we to stop him?

Iris's argument was that the difference did indeed go deeper than that – far deeper – and went as follows. Up until the end of the sixteenth century, even global trading outfits like the Levant Company were guilds or partnerships, whose members pooled their resources to do things that none could accomplish in isolation. But then, on 24 September 1599, in a half-timbered building off Moorgate Fields not far from where Shakespeare was struggling to complete *Hamlet*, something momentous happened. A company was founded whose ownership was cut up into tiny pieces to be bought and sold freely and anonymously, like pieces of silver. One could own a piece of the new company without being involved in it, indeed without even telling anyone. The first global joint stock company was thus born – undoubtedly Tudor England's most revolutionary invention. Its name? The East India Company.

A contemporary commentator drew an analogy between the East India Company's ownership structure and the River Thames's splendid flux, which leaves it 'still the same river, though the parts which compose it are changing every instance'. Once the property rights over a firm become detached from the people that set it up and work in it, it becomes a corpus in flux. It acquires a liquid life of its own. It can grow out of any human proportion. Indeed, like a river, it becomes potentially immortal.

History, Iris said, is the constant struggle to accumulate power over others. Money buys the resources needed to amass such power, for a king as much as for Coca-Cola. The right to issue unlimited quantities of anonymously tradable shares, along with the institution of a liquid market for them, created something new: corporations with power so immense it dwarfed that of their countries of origin and could be deployed in faraway places assiduously to exploit people and resources.

Shareholding and well-governed share markets fired up history. Separating ownership from the rest of the East India Company's activities unleashed a fluid, irresistible force. Unchecked, the East India Company grew more powerful than the British state, answerable only to its shareholders. At home, its bureaucracy corrupted and largely controlled Her Majesty's government. Abroad, its 200,000-strong private army oversaw the destruction of well-functioning economies in Asia and a number of Pacific islands and ensured the systematic exploitation of their peoples.

The East India Company was no aberration, though. It was the template for many subsequent corporations, such as the Anglo-Persian Oil Company, which in 1953 marshalled the British and American secret services to overthrow the last democratically elected Iranian government. Or the communications conglomerate ITT, which played a major role in the murderous *coup d'état* in Chile twenty years later. Or indeed more recent mega-corporations like Amazon, Facebook, Google and ExxonMobil, which are effectively beyond the control of any nation state.

Liberals betray themselves, Iris argued, the moment they turn a blind eye to this kind of hyper-concentrated power. Freedom means as much in a society under the thumb of the East India Company as it does in those controlled by totalitarian regimes: nothing. This is why trading in apples does not even come close to trading in shares. Large quantities of apples may produce, at worst, lots of bad cider. But large amounts of money invested in liquid shares can release demonic forces that no market or state can control.

'Liberalism's fatal hypocrisy,' said Iris, 'was to rejoice in the virtuous Jills and Jacks, the neighbourhood butchers, bakers and brewers, so as to defend the vile East India Companies, the Facebooks and the Amazons, which know no neighbours, have no partners, respect no moral sentiments and stop at nothing to destroy their competitors. By replacing partnerships with anonymous shareholders, we created Leviathans that end up undermining and defying all the values that liberals like you, Eva, claim to cherish.'

In spite of herself, and roused in part by her own words, Iris found herself warming to the world Kosti described in his dispatches.

Going with the evolutionary flow or dallying with extinction?

'You're clutching at straws, Iris,' Eva said, with an undisguised look of pity on her face. 'The beauty of markets is that they are the natural habitat in which the fittest organizational forms survive. Anything else exists only in fiction. If democratic corporations, based on a one-person-one-share rule, were better in any sense, they would exist in the here and now. As it is, they exist only in Costa's fantastical dispatches.'

Costa took this as his cue. 'That a system evolved in a given environment only proves it's best at replicating itself in that environment,' he said. 'That doesn't make it a system that we should want to live in. Nor, more importantly, is it any indication of its ability to survive over the longer term. Environments change, sometimes rapidly, sometimes because of the system's own ill effects. Outcompeting other systems, rather than living harmoniously with them, can eventually be self-destructive. Viruses are a good case in point. The Ebola virus, though extremely infectious and good at replicating itself, kills its hosts much more frequently than, say, Covid-19. The fact that coronavirus was relatively harmless is what allowed it to bring capitalism to its knees in 2020. The question is not whether share trading and capitalism have outcompeted other systems up until now but whether their effects are consistent with their host's survival! And for that, we need to take into account a factor that neither of you have yet considered.'

'Is that so, Costa?' said Eva. 'Well, then. Be so kind as to tell us. What have we overlooked?'

'Technology, of course,' he answered.

Electrified liquidity

'If we are properly to assess the effects of share markets today,' Costa went on, 'we cannot confine ourselves to their birth back in the seventeenth century, as Iris has done, or to the mere fact of their prevalence, as you have done, Eva. We must consider how they have evolved in relation with their environment. The introduction of tradable shares might have made companies limitless in theory, but it's only with the invention of specific technologies that they have become limitless in practice: the technologies made possible by the discovery and harnessing of electromagnetism by James Clerk Maxwell in 1865.

'Now, I happily concede that if Maxwell had come up with his equations in, say, the fifteenth century, they would have excited only a few fellow mathematicians. Nothing more. It took Thomas Edison to turn those equations into the kind of electricity grid that would eventually power the world, and Edison would never have been able to do this without the vast sums of money made accessible to him by share markets. I'm sure I don't need to remind you, Eva, that his Pearl Street Station, the first electric utility provider, was shareholder-owned.'

'My point precisely.' Eva smiled. 'Without Maxwell's equations, of course there would be no electric power generation, no telephony, no radar, lasers or anything digital at all. But without the share market to provide the massive funding necessary to build the networked firms – the General Electrics, the Bell Corporations, the Amazons – the scientists' blueprints would remain in museums, along with Leonardo da Vinci's helicopter designs. This is why I think it is pure madness to imagine an advanced society that bans share markets.'

'But hold on, Eva,' Costa cautioned. 'When share markets met technology, they didn't stay the same. They transformed one another, they evolved. Together they created something new: the Technostructure. And in the process they changed their environment too.'

The birth of the Technostructure

The real force that pushed history to breakneck velocity, Costa explained, was not the share market. Share markets were simply not liquid enough to bankroll Edison-sized ambitions. At the turn of the twentieth century, he reminded Eva, neither the banks nor the share markets could raise the kind of money needed to build all those power stations, grids, factories and distribution networks. To get those vast projects off the ground, what was required was an equivalently sized network of credit.

Hand in hand, shareholding and technology led to the creation of shareholder-owned mega-banks willing to lend to the new mega-firms by generating a new kind of mega-debt. This took the form of vast overdraft facilities for the Thomas Edisons and the Henry Fords of the world. Of course, the money they were lent did not actually exist – yet. Rather, it was as if they were borrowing the future profits of their mega-firms in order to fund those mega-firms' construction.

The rivers of money these credit lines generated did much more than build the Bessemer furnaces, the pipelines, the machines, the transmitters and the cables. They paid also for mergers and acquisitions that generated industrial cartels far larger than the original networked mega-firms. A Soviet-like, albeit privately owned, planned system emerged, spanning

the globe, allowing the captains of industry and the masters
of finance, together, to shape the future for themselves and
in their image. This, explained Costa, is what John Kenneth
Galbraith called Technostructure, and is what, according to
Kosti, the techno-syndicalists of the Other Now sought to
bring down.

'Time and again over the course of the twentieth century,'
Costa said, 'the Technostructure grew beyond our control,
overwhelming any notion of market discipline or public virtue.
Like a virus, it has repeatedly sickened its host. Its extravagant
appetite for private debt caused the great crash of 1929, the
Depression of the 1930s and ultimately the calamity of the
Second World War. In its aftermath, post-war governments
neutered the mega-banks and placed the Technostructure on
a leash. But in the early 1970s, the Technostructure escaped
its leash and shook off all state restraints, aided and abetted by
Thatcher and Reagan's political insurgency.

'Once it was back in full control, the Technostructure's
plundering of future value reached new heights, causing
another great crash in 2008. This time, without the rubble of
a world war to clean up, it took no time at all for us to revive
the Technostructure with rivers of new public money printed
by the central banks. But by now, the virus had so sickened its
host, had so plundered its own environment, that a full recovery
was impossible. Bloated and inflamed, the Technostructure
was unable to convert the new liquidity into real productive
capacity, into good-quality jobs, into a carbon-neutral
economy drawing on planet-saving new forms of energy.
It took an actual virus in 2020, produced by environmental
pillaging, for most of us to realize the terrifying precariousness
of our situation. And yet, once again, governments saw fit to

pump trillions back into the Technostructure, clinging to the source of our sickness as if it were a life raft. By 2023, the Technostructure and its controlling oligarchs were in greater control than ever of a planet gripped by an out-of-control environmental and social crisis. So I fear that a ban on share-trading may not be sufficient for restoring sanity on planet earth,' concluded Costa. 'But, if you ask me, the OC rebels were damned right: it is necessary!'

The baby and the bathwater

Eva was not averse to this criticism of capitalism – namely, that it tended to favour big business – nor to criticism of mega-banks like Lehman for creating unstable debt mountains dwarfing Mount Everest. Free markets were her obsession, matched only by her fear of collectivism – not defending Goldman Sachs shenanigans or Amazon's right to destroy small businesses or ExxonMobil's incineration of the planet.

After all, she knew first hand what they had been up to. How chief executive officers had metamorphosed into financial gurus in order to appropriate, instead of add to, society's riches. Even before the crash of 2008, she had noted that sixty-five out of the one hundred wealthiest entities on earth were financialized corporations, not states. 'And believe you me,' she told her friends, 'these guys are not exactly custodians of society's values.'

'I don't need to be lectured on the perils of so much power in the hands of so few, corruptible businessmen,' she replied to Costa. 'But – and this is a huge but – throwing the baby out with the bathwater, is that wise? The fact that share markets facilitate the birth of public enemies, such as the East India

Company, Lehman or Walmart, is not a serious reason to ban tradable shares. Sure, cars can cause pile-ups. That's not a reason to ban them. It is, rather, a reason to enforce better road rules more rigorously. So too with corporations. By all means let society step in with the right carrots and sticks to steer them in the direction of the common interest.'

'Hang on, hang on.' Costa jumped at the chance to point out a rare inconsistency in Eva's argument. 'For as long as I've known you, you have challenged the very notion of a common interest.'

Eva winced. She was, indeed, one of those economists who believed that working out objectively what society wanted was not just difficult but in fact impossible. Put technically, Eva and economists of her ilk rejected the possibility of *any* impartial method for synthesizing the conflicting preferences of different people into one, sensible, actionable list of social priorities. This is why they believed that free market competition was the only reasonable and most efficient way to allocate resources. Indeed, it was this radical rejection of the idea of a common interest that Margaret Thatcher was alluding to when in an interview for *Woman's Own* in September 1987, she had asked rhetorically, 'Who is society? There is no such thing! There are individual men and women and there are families.'

'If it is impossible to define the common interest, society's collective will, as you have been telling us and your students for years,' continued Costa, 'then how will society step in? Towards what common objective will it steer the corporations? Or have you had a change of heart?'

'You are not wrong, Costa,' Eva admitted after a momentary pause. 'Every attempt to discern society's will is condemned to leave room for manipulation by some groups and individuals who are more influential than others. But, while our sense of the common interest is always imperfect, we can approximate it sufficiently well – and we must, so as to avoid losing the wealth-creating power of markets altogether.'

'I won't allow it!' thundered Iris from the sidelines. 'I won't allow you to sacrifice your only saving grace. At least stick to your guns, Eva!'

For Iris, Eva's saving grace had always been her Thatcher-like clean break from woolly, pseudo-progressive do-gooders who went on and on about the 'common interest' not realizing that they were simply defending a moribund status quo. Indeed, Iris wholly supported Eva's ruthless disavowal of the idea of common priorities, albeit for entirely opposing reasons.

'How can there be common ground,' Iris said, 'between a girl living without clean water on less than a dollar a day and one of those masters of the universe whose bonus alone is larger than the entire education budget of a sub-Saharan country?'

'And yet you can't have fair competition between them either, can you?' said Costa. 'No one can win against corporations as powerful as Amazon or Walmart.'

'There is only one choice,' continued Iris. 'Either we must surrender to an oligarchy that, in liberalism's name, steamrollers every value or freedom that matters. Or we must recognize that the invention of capitalism must be reversed, leaving only one road available to us: the one that, if Kosti is to be believed, the OC rebels paved in the Other Now.'

'Very well,' said Eva. 'I agree. You are probably right. Trying to tame the capitalist beast is probably futile. And in that case,' she said, staring Iris straight in the eye, 'in the same way you would have chosen Thatcher over the decrepit centrists in the early 1980s, I now choose the freedom to trade shares – even if this means my son will grow old in a world ruled by ugly, over-powerful corporations. There are no clean choices, Iris. We all have to choose our poison, the unfreedoms that we must live with. I choose not to live in a society that stops me from selling a share of my small business or from purchasing a tiny share in a large one. And I'll tell you why: because in the end, it's what lifted us all out of poverty and offers the only realistic prospect of doing the same for the millions who still suffer it.'

A fool's wager?

'Look around you, Iris,' Eva went on. 'Sure, 2008 was awful. But only middle-class hypocrites can fail to marvel at the technological progress of the past century, to feel the relief of billions who have been lifted from poverty in that time and who can now aspire to a multitude of advantages, from cheap clothes and plentiful food to a smartphone connecting them with the rest of humanity. It has all been made possible because share trading allowed the present to borrow from the future to make a better life for itself than in the past. Without that, companies must rely exclusively on loans for every bit of their funding, as they do in Kosti's Other Now. If that were the case, we'd still be living as we did in the sixteenth century.'

'Did you seriously learn nothing from 2008?' Iris asked. 'A licence to lend non-existing money, when combined with a share market, is the highway to ruin. Not only does it concentrate ownership of every business in the hands of a tiny minority, it fundamentally destabilizes the economy. Why? Because the future is a fool's wager, Eva! The future is a possibility, a who knows? or at best a perhaps. By deluding us with debt, capitalism has ensured that the future is not what it used to be. Five years ago, Covid-19 pricked our debt bubble, exposing capitalism's incredible fragility. It put to bed all the nonsense about our recovery from 2008. All capitalism proved itself capable of after 2020 – just as after 2008 – was a fascinating reversal of natural selection: the larger an institution's failure and the steeper its financial losses, the greater its capacity to appropriate society's surplus via massive bailouts. Capitalism, thy name is bankruptocracy – rule by the most bankrupt of bankers!'

Eva was unperturbed. 'This capitalist Technostructure, as Costa refers to it,' she replied, 'why deny its great achievements? The way it transformed China into a powerhouse, harnessed millions of brilliant Indian technologists, ended food shortages in most of Africa, made it possible for people with no bank account to send and receive money using their mobile phones. For all its obvious failures, is it wise to jeopardize these achievements with a ban on share trading?'

Costa interrupted, sensing an impasse. Once again, he felt his two friends were missing the wider picture.

'Corporations go to great lengths to employ geniuses: technologists, designers, financial engineers, economists, artists even. I've seen it happen,' he said. 'But what have they done with them? They channel all that talent and creativity towards humanity's destruction. Even when it is creative, Eva, capitalism is extractive. In search of shareholder profit, corporations have put these geniuses in charge of extracting the last morsel of value from humans and from the earth, from the minerals in its guts to the life in its oceans. And these brilliant minds have been used to cajole governments into accepting their raids on the planet's resources by creating markets for them: markets for carbon dioxide and other pollutants – phoney markets controlled by their employers! Unlike the East India Company, the Technostructure does not need its own armies. It owns our states and their armies, because it controls what we think. The dirtier the industry, the richer and more despised, the more its captains have been able to tap into the rivers of debt-derived money to purchase influence and to blunt opposition. Previously they would buy newspapers and set up TV stations; now they employ armies of lobbyists, found think tanks, litter the Internet with their trolls and, of course, direct monumental campaign donations to the chief enablers of our species' extinction, the politicians.'

'Costa is right, Eva,' said Iris. 'The future is a fool's wager and the greatest fools are those aiding and abetting a Technostructure betting on our future. A modern Prospero would have hailed the fate of fictitious wealth to "melt into air, into thin air". In 2008 it was finance that melted down. In 2020 it was every market on the planet, except those for ventilators, sanitisers and toilet paper. By 2023 the point of no return from climate calamity had come and gone, with the world's last glaciers almost totally melted.'

Capitalism-induced climate change upset Eva even more than it did her friends. Unlike them, she had a son to whom she felt she was bequeathing a dying planet. Except that she did not think that anything good would come from ending capitalism. To reverse capitalism's catastrophic effects on nature and the planet's climate, she believed, lots of cash is needed. Which means we need share markets guided to fund green investments, directed by a proper tax on bad stuff, for instance carbon dioxide and other threats to our habitat.

'Have you forgotten, Eva, the old maxim that the house can't be beaten?' came Iris's admonition. 'No matter how many markets you design, or simulate, irrespectively of how many new taxes you introduce, once Capitalism Inc. bets on our future, we have no future. Why is human life unsustainable today? Because smart people like you continue to defend shareholding even though you know that the right to buy into a future profit stream reinforces the irrepressible Technostructure and dissolves all its restraints. Congratulations, sister. You have enabled them to double down on our extinction!'

'Whatever you say about capitalism,' Eva retorted, 'every alternative is guaranteed to be worse. This is why capitalism is perceived by most people as inevitable.'

'So was, once, the divine right of kings. Until it wasn't,' said Costa.

'Sure,' said Eva, 'but do you really believe that flat management and single, non-tradable shares will do the trick? That they will produce a green revolution capable of saving our species' bacon?'

'I am not sure, Eva,' Costa confessed, 'but I trust that what Kosti is describing comes the closest to a realistic utopia worth fighting for.'

'Do you know what my problem with any utopia is, Costa?' Iris asked sternly. 'Men! Like everything that has a potential to be beautiful, you men try to take it over and turn it into something vile. And, what's worse, most women defer to you in the process.'

Eva remained silent.

The cafeteria controversy

Markets without capitalism was not a bridge too far for Eva. In fact, she liked the sound of it, even if she remained entirely sceptical about what it would entail in practice. But she had an ethical objection, too, which she now put to her companions.

'Suppose you and I start a cafe. We put plenty of work and loving care into it, not to mention money. Then we need to hire some help, say a person to wait tables in the afternoons. Are you seriously telling me that it would be acceptable for the state to compel us to hand over an equal share in our cafe to some random waiter that we hire? That the state should have the right to hand this person decision-making powers equal to yours and mine? And can you please answer the question without first giving me another historical diatribe?'

Lest she be seen to be doing what she was told, Iris muttered something about 'a widespread mental failure to recognize the unacceptability of thinking of people as bundles of labour for hire. But since you demand a yes or no answer,' she went on, 'I shall give you one: yes, I do think it is perfectly fine, indeed necessary, for the state to compel us to give the waiter equal decision-making powers. Put it this way. I agree, Eva, that you and I cannot be equal in any mathematical sense. Our contribution, talents and energy are inevitably unequal. And yet you are happy with the idea of sharing ownership of the cafe fifty-fifty with me, correct? If the shares can be divided between us perfectly equally, why not with the waiter too?'

'Well, for three obvious reasons, at least,' responded Eva coolly. 'First, you and I came up with the idea of the cafe together and put in the hard work to make it a reality, whereas the waiter arrived on the scene later on. Second, we invested equal sums of money, unlike the waiter. And third, having invested so much less time, money and social capital in the whole enterprise, there is no way the waiter could possibly have the same commitment to it as we would.'

'You and I might have come up with the idea,' responded Iris, 'and we might have done the initial hard work, but a business lives and dies day by day. The moment the waiter enters the scene, she begins to make a daily contribution that may be unequal to ours but is every bit as important. Besides, do we really want ownership to be determined on a first-come-first-served basis? What if the waiter ends up bringing in a whole load of new customers that you and I could never have attracted ourselves? Your second reason is more powerful, though, I admit. However, suppose we agree that shares should be distributed in proportion to the money a partner injects into the business – that they should be purchased, in effect – surely it is only right that we should also be able to sell them on, irrespective of whether we continue to work in the cafe or not? But the moment we allow someone who doesn't work in the cafe to buy into it, it's finished. It'll close or end up as another miserable Starbucks, an appendage of the Technostructure.'

Eva's third reason, Iris thought, was the most compelling but not a clincher either.

'Even if the waiter was less committed,' she went on, 'you and I would still retain the majority of the cafeteria's shares, allowing us to fire the waiter or to reduce the waiter's bonuses. And if this means we take extra care when hiring a second or third waiter, to avoid a coalition of the unworthy, that would be only good and proper. The pressing question,' Iris told her friend, 'is not really who owns which shares. After all, equal shares do not mean equal rewards. But they are the only real way of acknowledging and dealing with what you have been saying for yonks: that it is impossible objectively to measure personal contributions to a joint endeavour. Isn't this why when we publish academic work we opt for the convention of joint authorship and alphabetical listing of our names?'

'I'm always glad to see lefties abandon the dangerous idea that persons are equal in any meaningful way,' Eva said good-humouredly.

'Right, so we need to refocus, away from the question of who owns how many shares and on to what effect that would have. The real question is: do we want the net revenues of an enterprise to be distributed by a workplace dictatorship, which is inevitable if shares are traded? Or do we want the division of a firm's loot to be decided by a workplace democracy, which is only possible if there are equally distributed and non-tradable shares?'

They had got to the kernel of the issue.

'You're right, Iris,' said Eva. 'I vote for capitalism and tradable shares knowing full well that it's a vote for a dictatorship in the workplace – but it's an internal dictatorship from which anyone can resign and the prerequisite for liberty at large.'

'And I vote,' said Iris, smiling, 'for a democratic workplace – the only type that does not make a mockery of liberal democracy and a wasteland out of our planet.'

It was the closest the two of them would get to an alignment of views, and Eva was tempted at that point to step back from any further argument. But they had yet to address what was to her mind the Other Now's vilest institution: the Socialworthiness Index and the Citizens' Juries, which had the power to dissolve corporations if, in their estimation, they did not serve the public good.

'Can you imagine a worse tyranny,' Eva asked, 'than living in fear of some random jury passing judgement over us and closing our cafe?'

'I agree with Sartre: hell is other people,' Costa stepped in to reply. 'But of all the ways our life can be made hellish, such juries seem far preferable to credit-rating agencies, to markets dominated by an imperial Technostructure, or indeed to the surveillance of big tech, turning us, via our data, into its products.'

Iris thought it was the right moment to bring China into the conversation. 'I gather that the Chinese communist party tells its nation's business owners that their shares will be appropriated if they fail to serve society. I would rather die than trust any elected body, let alone a communist party, with that power. But in the end, no one has the divine right to own anything, so we have to decide somehow, and I'd rather a random selection of my fellow citizens made that call than anyone else. Indeed, I can think of no better check on power, public or private.'

And so the debate went on. Iris oscillated between playing devil's advocate and arguing strongly in support of both the plausibility and the attractiveness of the Other Now. Eva maintained a fascinated hostility towards it. One moment she was enthused by the idea of central banks offering personal accounts and a universal income to citizens, the next she was poking fun at the idea that companies should pay tax on their revenues rather than their profits. Occasionally Iris would take aim at Costa and his unreconstructed egalitarianism – and on those occasions Eva could not help but agree with her. Costa, meanwhile, jet-lagged and content to turn spectator, dozed off on the couch while their battle of wits continued well into the night.

The sabbatical

In the morning, he woke to find Iris and Eva exhausted but still deep in debate. Over the next three days, they continued to meet and argue, and all the while Costa busily took notes, equipping himself with questions to put to Kosti upon his return to San Francisco. The evening before he was due to catch his flight, Eva and Iris had sat down with him to finalize the list of questions he would ask. But when the day of his departure came, as they sat sharing a last cup of tea, Iris and Eva told him they were not yet ready for him to leave.

In what was for Costa a precious show of unity, they confessed to having been energized by his extraordinary claims and the intricate thought experiment he had unleashed. Iris had relished revisiting some of the most contentious topics of her past, she told him. Eva, meanwhile, felt unexpectedly relieved to have been able to express her views on the deleterious impact of big business. 'I owe a debt of gratitude,' she said, 'to the prankster who has convinced you he's your alternative self.'

'How can you be so sure that it's all a hoax, though?' asked Costa.

'Besides the implausible physics? I just don't buy it – that the masses could ever coordinate to bring capitalism down. Digital solidarity, your so-called OC rebellion, leading to a world-changing bloodless revolution … It all sounds great, but so does the idea of fairies at the bottom of the garden. Even so, we'll be sad to see you go.'

'The physics is entirely real, I assure you. As for the politics, well, no revolution seems plausible until it happens. But just think of what crowd-sourced action has achieved here in Our Now. There was the nurses' strike in Portugal in 2019 – funded by tens of thousands of supporters until they won against the government. Before that, in Finland, thousands participated in a universal basic income experiment for two whole years, donating serious money to perfect strangers. In New Zealand, a group of hackers even planned to target CDOs in a very similar way to the Crowdshorters. Why, in the midst of the 2020 pandemic, a centenarian crowd-funded over thirty million quid for your NHS just by walking round his garden! Had any of those campaigns extended beyond helping the weak and actually taken aim at punishing the financiers responsible for the economic crisis, or the corporations for destroying the planet, or the governments for failing to protect us against disease – then I'd wager that anything is possible.'

It was clear from the look on Eva's face that she was not convinced. Costa now startled both himself and his friends with a suggestion. 'Why don't the two of you return with me, to San Francisco, to interrogate *your* alter egos.'

As soon as he'd said it, it seemed the obvious thing to do. Cerberus' security made it possible to exchange messages only between senders sharing the exact same DNA. Costa was therefore constrained to converse only with Kosti, who seemed exhausted by their exchanges. But there was no technical reason why Iris and Eva could not send questions to their counterparts, assuming they were alive and well in the Other Now and that Kosti could track them down.

'I'm sure you have a million things to ask them that Kosti could never know,' Costa said.

Eva turned to Iris, who stared silently at the kitchen floor for some time. When eventually she looked up and met Eva's gaze, Costa knew their answer.

'Maybe I could get Thomas to join us,' Eva said quietly.

Thomas had been living in the United States for the last two years, since dropping out of school after his GCSEs, and Eva hadn't seen him in all that time. He avoided contact, telling his mother only that he was trying to reconnect with his dad and 'find' himself away from her. Whenever his name was inadvertently mentioned, Eva could not help but sigh. But on this occasion she had mentioned his name brightly. Maybe she could interest him in a trip to Silicon Valley, a chance to spend time in a cutting-edge laboratory, perhaps even a peek down a real wormhole …

'I should warn you, though,' said Costa. 'Stare into the wormhole and you risk seeing some hard, intimate truths.'

'What do you mean?' asked Iris.

'Just before I flew out to see you, Kosti referred in passing to someone called Cleo, saying he adores her. It turns out, she's his daughter.' Costa paused, took a sip of tea and let out a sigh. 'The bastard has a life!' Turning to his two friends, he added, 'I hope you're readier than I was for such surprises.'

6

Markets Without Capitalism

More personal than political

Agreeing on which questions each would send down the wormhole was easy. But coming up with a plan for introducing Iris and Eva to Siris and Eve, the nicknames Costa had given their Other Now selves, was not.

On his return to San Francisco, Costa had put their idea to Kosti, who had leaped at it. He had remained in close touch with his old friend Siris, and he had a good idea how to track down Eve, who, as it happened, was a prominent figure in the Other Now. In fact, Kosti had already begun to consider how he might bring them in on the secret. Inspired by Costa's successful trip to Brighton, he said he would try it. A week later, he wrote to say that Siris and Eve were sceptical but game, though they would need much convincing that any of this was real. A week after that, at the beginning of June, Iris and Eva arrived in California, where they were now holed up in Costa's lab, sharing a spacious room two doors down the corridor from HALPEVAM's main installation. They were now about to contact persons with whom they had supposedly shared a life until September 2008. The opening missives would be vital for convincing both parties that the wormhole was real and for establishing trust.

'Before you ask any questions,' Costa advised them, 'make sure to mention something that only you would know, to establish credibility. It's how I got Kosti to believe me in the first place, too.'

Eva liked it that her friends thought of Lehman's collapse in September 2008 as her lowest point. It helped camouflage her true nadir – the end of her relationship with Thomas's father, shortly after she had arrived at Princeton pregnant with his child. Financial ruin and the disintegration of her mind's model of the world paled into irrelevance compared to the realization that she meant nothing to him, having thought she meant everything. It was a trauma she had shared with no one.

'Do you still feel the loss of him as I do?' she asked Eve.

While waiting for Eve's reply, she grew aghast at how needy she must have sounded, and at how inexplicably desolate she had felt ever since he disappeared. When the answer came, Eva did not know whether to feel relieved or ashamed: Eve hardly remembered him.

Surprise turned quickly into sheer curiosity. 'What of Thomas?' Eva asked. Tears filled her eyes as she read Eve's reply. There was no Thomas in the Other Now; but there was Agnes, her nine-year-old daughter. Iris was fond of reminding Eva of the 1970s feminist slogan, 'The personal is political.' Now it struck her that the opposite was true as well.

Like reunited identical twins, Eva and Eve delved into each other's pasts, eager to learn what could have been. Eva opened her heart first, describing how Lehman's bankruptcy had stunned her into a long period of inactivity, from which Thomas's father alone was able sporadically to rouse her. How eventually, and despite him, she overcame her lethargy by applying to Princeton for a place on their economics doctoral programme. How he would not leave her alone, exploiting her vulnerability to him. How he then fled upon learning of her pregnancy. How she had given birth to Thomas among strangers. How she had struggled as a single mum to complete a tough PhD. How she had decided to escape to Brighton.

Eve repaid her amply, describing how his spell lifted quickly thanks to an email that landed in her in-box in November 2008, sent by someone calling herself Esmeralda. It was not a personal email but one addressed to the many Wall Street analysts who had just lost their jobs. Esmeralda was inviting them to join the Crowdshorters – the band of financial engineers who, ultimately, would use Wall Street's weapons to bring down the CDO-derivatives market and, with it, the investment banks. Racked with guilt about having taken part in the massive fraud that had passed as investment banking, Eve was tempted. When she told her partner, he was furious. Having been her boss at Lehman, he still felt entitled to order her about. Her choice was clear: a lowly job as a member of the incoming Obama task force whose job was to re-float Wall Street and which he was to lead. Or join Esmeralda's Crowdshorters. It was no choice at all.

And so Eve had found herself in the midst of the OC rebellion. As Barack Obama was moving into the White House, Eve was becoming an integral member of the Crowdshorters' East Coast team. Her Lehman experience proved handy in unpicking the derivatives that the authorities were trying to revive in order to rebuild the empire of finance that had just imploded. 'We lived in thrilling times. Nothing like a high-tech revolution to sharpen the mind and dissolve loneliness,' was how she described it to Eva.

A year later, Eve hooked up with Ebo, a fellow Crowdshorter who had begun his revolutionary career working with Akwesi's Bladerunners in Ghana. He had come to New York to work on a joint campaign to incite a series of payment strikes while also targeting the financial instruments whose underlying payment streams the strike would weaken. As the OC revolution bore fruit, Eve and Ebo worked all hours to help set up the Other Now's new institutions.

Ebo rose to lead the Human Movement Project, an international agency helping people migrate. Eve, drawing on her financial background, worked for the International Monetary Project – the successor to the International Monetary Fund – which regulated the world's currency system. But all work took a back seat when their baby girl, Agnes, arrived in 2016. On that day Esmeralda sent Eve a handwritten note that read, 'May she grow up a cheerful enemy of repression.'

Eva smiled when she learned this. The thought that Thomas had a half-sister of sorts was surprisingly comforting.

Plumbers versus waiters

As the days and then weeks passed, their correspondence inevitably turned political. The first question Eva asked was to do with the subject that had preoccupied her most since reading Kosti's dispatches: the fact that firms could not hire anyone without making them equal partners first.

'Surely when you want a minor role filled, you must be able to hire someone in return for nothing more than a sum of money?' she asked.

'Sure,' answered Eve, 'as long as the task meets the Disjointedness Criterion.'

She explained that the Disjointedness Criterion, or DC for short, had been introduced in the Other Now to distinguish between value production that requires teamwork and value that can be created and measured individually. For example, when a plumber is called in to fix a burst pipe, the work performed can be valued separately from any work others do in the same building. Thus, DC applies here and plumbers have no right to demand a share of the firm – they are just paid for the service provided.

In contrast, actors bring to a play their individual panache, talent, commitment. One or two bring star quality to the stage, stimulating demand for tickets. Some have substantial roles that make them look good. A few are mere extras. Nevertheless, every play is an example of joint production in the sense that it is impossible objectively to measure the contribution of each participant, from individual actors to the director, the set designer, the lighting director and the many others involved. Here DC does not apply. In such teamwork-based enterprises, the one-person-one-share-one-vote rule holds because of the impossibility of measuring objectively individual contributions. Different individual contributions are of course rewarded with different bonuses. However, they do not legitimize different degrees of ownership.

'What about a casual waiter in a cafe?' asked Eva. 'Does the DC not apply there?'

'No, it doesn't,' answered Eve. 'Unlike casual plumbers, waiters are part of the cafe's culture, its product.' In addition to fetching cups of coffee, she explained, they partake in producing the atmosphere that customers pay for. So too in an office, in a factory, on a farm, in an architect's studio – wherever the final product reflects the culture of the workplace and the synergies between all participants, DC does not apply.

'But it seems crazy to introduce such a ludicrous degree of inflexibility into the market for labour,' Eva said. 'Surely it puts a huge constraint on the willingness and capacity of companies to take on new staff.'

'But this is where you're wrong,' replied Eve. 'No such thing as a labour market can exist or indeed ever existed.'

Even under capitalism, Eve insisted, the moment someone is hired they leave the market and enter its opposite: a planned system – the firm. In any marketplace, especially the digital one, you simply buy and sell, often anonymously. Beyond the financial transaction, there is no relationship with your counterparty. Once you join a company, by contrast, you cooperate, cajole, propose, argue, support, vow, inspire, form coalitions, moan about colleagues – in short, you enter a *relationship* unregulated by prices, just like a marriage or joining the army or forming a theatre company. The only difference between capitalism and the Other Now, Eve continued, is the type of relationships workers experience. Under capitalism, relations within a firm are despotic, as is the distribution of its net revenues. Under the Other Now's corpo-syndicalism, relations are democratic. And so is the distribution of bonuses.

Unsatisfied but realizing that she had hit a wall, Eva decided reluctantly to move on to one of the many other questions she wanted to ask. It was a big one.

Money

In Eva's university lectures, money was the hardest thing to explain even to the smartest of students. In fact, it had taken Eva herself months of working in Wall Street to escape fully her own misconception of how money is created. As a physics major, before getting her hands dirty in New York, she had assumed that money is printed by a nation's central bank, from where it is distributed to commercial banks. But while this is indeed how cash is created, cash accounts for only 3 per cent of all money. What of the remaining 97 per cent?

Surprise and then foreboding were the reactions of every student to whom she had explained how the missing 97 per cent was created – and by whom: not by central banks but by commercial and investment bankers. At this point, her students would ask, 'Without access to state-sanctioned printing presses, how do private bankers create money?'

'Simple,' she would reply. 'Every time a banker approves a loan of, say, one million dollars for Jack, a typical business customer, the banker just types 1,000,000 on Jack's bank statement. However incredible it may seem, that's all it takes. Bankers create money by granting loans by typing in some numbers!'

The crucial thing, she would explain, is that these numbers are typed into a shared database – or ledger – to which only the bankers have access. When their customers transfer this 'money' between them – when Jack transfers numbers from his account to the account of a supplier, say Jill, or of a builder, say Bob, or of a worker, say Kate, and when in turn, Jill, Bob and Kate transfer their numbers on, in the same way, to others to whom they owe money – these numbers simply migrate from one cell in the database to another. For this system to be sustainable, and not merely a pyramid scheme, there is a single condition: that, somewhere down the line, the one million dollars which some banker typed into existence on Jack's behalf results in new goods and services whose total market value exceeds one million dollars. It is from this surplus that the banker takes his interest and Jack his profit. This is what Iris was referring to as a fool's wager when she said that bankers plundered value from the future, or when Costa had once claimed that capitalism, like science fiction, trades in future assets using fictitious currency.

It is in their nature that the wealthier bankers become by creating money, the more money they tend to create. The danger of such a system, of course, is that the banks end up typing into existence sums of money vastly larger than the market value of the goods and services created as a result of Jack, Jill, Bob and Kate's endeavours. At the point when the bankers have collectively created money sums greater than the resulting values, the present can no longer repay the future for the money it borrowed from it. The moment Jack, Jill, Bob and Kate get a whiff of this, they may demand their bank balances in cash, sensing that the total value on the bankers' database is lower than the actual value of their customers' assets.

'At that point, a bank run sets in,' Eva would tell her students, 'and that's when the system comes crashing down.'

In capitalism's Wild West, also known as the market for money and credit, the central bank plays sheriff to restrain bankers from flooding the world with unlimited quantities of money and causing bank runs. It does so by pointing at them a double-barrelled gun. One barrel contains the threat that the central bank might not lend to them during a bank run. The second barrel is loaded with increases in the interest rate it will charge them if it does lend to them. Upping the interest rate, or threatening altogether to cut off bankers who lend too much, are the two means that central banks have of restraining bankers' tendency to breed more and more money. The trick is to get the balance just right: allow bankers enough leeway for the economy to be able to grow, but not so much that the influx of money outpaces the production of new goods, causing each pound or dollar to be worth less in real terms – known as inflation.

What was now uppermost in Eva's mind was the information from Kosti's dispatches that banks had become redundant after the OC revolution for two reasons. One was the demise of share markets, which under capitalism were the cause of a large percentage of the money created by the private banks. The other, crucially, was the provision by central banks of a PerCap account to every resident, comprising three free accounts: Legacy (a trust fund for every baby), Dividend (the depository of one's universal basic dividends) and Accumulation (a standard savings account in which all private earnings accumulated). All this seemed straightforward enough to Eva, but she could not understand two things. How did PerCap come into being? And how did the central bank regulate the total supply of money in order to allow for growth but not let inflation get out of hand? Did it simply increase the Dividend, for example, to increase the amount of money in the system? If the only loans available to businesses came from individuals and were backed by savings, did it just dictate an increase in the interest rates lenders had to charge if the central bank wanted to cool the economy down? Did the central bank, in other words, have a complete monopoly on money creation and loans – indeed, all finance? Wasn't such a concentration of power incredibly dangerous, not to mention inefficient? Eve's answers gave her a great deal of food for thought.

Eve explained that the migration from commercial bank accounts to the new central-bank-based banking system was gradual and ran at different speeds in different places. In the United States it began in 2012 and was completed in 2018. In

Britain it began a little later and was completed in 2019. In Europe, Latin America, India and other jurisdictions it took longer still. China moved most swiftly and had implemented its own version by the end of 2012.

It started in the United States as an attempt to show people that the Fed, the nation's central bank, had their backs. In early 2011, as the OC rebellion was taking root, anyone with a social security number was given a Fed account called Personal Capital, their PerCap. It started small, with the Fed crediting small amounts, around two hundred dollars, to each account every month. That money could not be taken out as cash but it could be transferred to any other PerCap account freely, using a PIN, and could also be used to pay taxes. It was therefore accepted as payment by anyone who had to pay taxes or who transacted with people or companies who paid taxes – effectively everyone!

People used up those small amounts fairly quickly to pay taxes but also each other. But because their PerCap monthly sum was small, people still relied mainly on their commercial bank accounts. To encourage people to transfer their savings from the commercial banks to their PerCap account at the Fed, the authorities made them an attractive offer. First, they created a second account for everyone, which they called Accumulation to differentiate it from their original account, which they now called Dividend. 'Here's the deal,' residents in the United States were told: 'For every $1000 you transfer to your PerCap Accumulation account, you can save up to $50, or 5 per cent, in taxes as long as you keep the money there for a year.' Put another way, Americans were offered 5 per cent tax relief if they paid their tax a year in advance, while still retaining the right to change their minds and spend it in the meantime. Given that commercial banks could never afford to offer their customers a 5 per cent interest rate on their savings, and lacked the right to offer tax relief, money began to migrate from commercial bank accounts to people's PerCap Accumulation accounts at the Fed.

By offering customers debit cards and smartphone apps with their PerCap Dividend and Accumulation accounts, most were enticed to shift their money to the Fed. The initial lure was the prospect of earning 5 per cent tax relief – in essence, 5 per cent interest – but it was also the lack of fees, bureaucracy and fuss that attracted them. Once they had transferred their savings from commercial banks to Accumulation accounts, people had no need to move their money from a current account to a special savings account to earn interest; there was no red tape, everything was done automatically. Why stick to commercial banks paying minuscule interest and charging transaction fees?

The next great enticement was when the Fed decreed that every newborn would be granted a Legacy account. Initially, this contained $100,000 – although, of course, it could not be used until the baby was an adult and had a plan for its use. Grateful parents, drawn by their kids' Legacy grants, began to use their PerCap accounts even more.

By 2019, most transactions had shifted from the bankers' joint database, or inter-bank payment system, to the Fed's books, where every PerCap sat. This new Fed-based, publicly owned alternative system was evolving organically into a formidable institution. A year earlier all personal and sales taxes had been abolished, however the authorities decided to maintain the 5 per cent effective interest rate as an incentive to people to save. How could this be done now that they could not offer them personal tax relief? Very simply: for every $100 dollars kept unspent in a PerCap, the account holder received an additional $5 twelve months hence. The Fed's all-inclusive public payment system soon became as loved and prized as the public libraries of yesteryear. It even acquired a suitable name for itself: Jerome, an inspired choice by one of the Crowdshorters who wanted to make a point after finding out that St Jerome was the patron saint of librarians. By 2020, Jerome, the Fed's database containing everyone's PerCap accounts (Legacy, Dividend and Accumulation), and allowing instantaneous free transfers between them, had driven into extinction the private for-fee inter-bank payment system that commercial bankers had controlled for centuries under capitalism.

Eva was impressed to discover that the OC rebels instinctively distrusted central banks, even after taking them over. Above the entrance to the Federal Reserve in Washington DC, Esmeralda's team had inscribed an unambiguous warning: BEWARE THE POWER TO CREATE MONEY FOR IT DOES TO ETHICS THAT WHICH WATER DOES TO SALT. As Eve explained, the OC rebels had in mind the way workers were short-changed by their governments in the early 1970s. The central banks had created such a wall of new money that even though workers were given pay rises, the actual value of their salaries fell because of rampant inflation.

To prevent Jerome from being abused by those in charge of it, the OC rebels imposed full transparency on their system. All transactions within Jerome were coordinated via an ingenious algorithm that, as Eve explained, allowed for every payment or transfer to be utterly private while, at the same time, everyone could see how much money sloshed around the system in aggregate. In other words, the authorities could not create more money – under, say, pressure from special interests – without everyone knowing.

Eva was impressed that leftist rebels could be worried about inflation, contrary to her assumption that such concerns were exclusive to liberal economists and conservative politicians. After all, Margaret Thatcher and Ronald Reagan had made their names by lambasting woolly centre-left governments for allowing inflation to run riot by printing money to curry favour with the trade unions and the poor.

However, the OC rebels' fears had a different source: the anarcho-syndicalist conviction that ethics dissolve when introduced to concentrated power and that those in charge of decision-making at central banks should therefore be protected from inevitable temptation. Her sympathy for the rebels growing with everything she learned, Eva wondered what the Other Now's anarcho-syndicalist central bankers would think if they knew how America, Britain and Europe's central banks had behaved after 2008, and indeed after 2020 – creating trillions of dollars, pounds and euros for the ultra-rich 0.1 per cent, while the masses drove themselves into the ground working for a pittance.

Another of Jerome's features that enthused Eva was its fully decentralized digital architecture. This mattered both technically and politically. Technically, it meant that all the payment data within Jerome would survive, should any part of it be damaged or destroyed. Politically, it mattered even more because it meant that no one had central access to or control over this information – not even the central bank. This type of distributed payments system sounded familiar to Eva. She asked Eve who had designed it.

'Apparently,' Eve replied, 'the computer code on which Jerome was eventually based appeared out of the blue in October 2008. It was posted in some Internet chat room by an anonymous hacker, I believe. It was signed In-Cognito, but whoever that was never came forward to claim the glory.'

That made sense, thought Eva. In-Cognito must be the same unidentified person or team who called themselves Satoshi Nakamoto, the inventor of Bitcoin. Their systems sounded identical. The difference, of course, was that in Our Now Bitcoin evolved into a pyramid scheme of hyper-speculation, whereas in the Other Now, where money and corporations were democratized, the system became the platform of a plain vanilla public payments system resembling the boring but ever-so-glorious public library.

Meanwhile, the introduction of corpo-syndicalist legislation, which ended tradable shares, had dealt the final blow to investment banking. Within a few years, cash and share markets were almost gone, and only digital money carrying the central bank's digital imprimatur and circulating from one PerCap to another remained legal tender. The end of commercial and investment banking did not, however, translate into the complete state monopoly of borrowing and lending that Eva feared. The opposite occurred.

Countless community-based outfits emerged offering loans, piggybacking on Jerome – the central bank's free digital payments system. These cooperative money brokers would pool the funds of savers who were eager to lend some of their PerCap Dividend or Accumulation, and would use this to lend to those corporations they identified as being more efficient, and thus bearing less risk, charging a modest commission from both sides. The two great differences between these money brokers and capitalist bankers were, first, that they themselves were shareholder-less partnerships and, more importantly, they could only loan value that had already been created and banked by persons and corporations – banned as they were from pillaging the future via overdraft facilities.

As for Eva's question regarding the total supply of money in the economy, the central bank's charter was clear. The quantity of money was adjusted constantly with a view to regulating prices and enabling the production of socially valued goods and services for society. When average prices rose above a certain threshold, the central bank would increase the interest it offered to people saving in their PerCaps, thereby encouraging the public to reduce spending. At other times, when economic activity was deemed too sluggish, the central bank would reduce the interest rate and/or increase the universal basic amount that it paid into all PerCap Dividend accounts.

When Eva asked if central banks remained independent of government, as the Fed or the Bank of England supposedly are in Our Now, she got a typically Other-Now-ish answer: central banks remained independent of government but not of society. Their monetary committees, which made all decisions relating to the supply of money, were appointed and supervised by a citizens' monetary assembly, comprising a rotating panel, chosen by lot, using an algorithm that ensured fair representation of all members of society.

Eva's initial terror at the idea of a state monopoly of financial services began to wane once she heard of the boisterous, decentralized market for credit. It abated further when she learned about citizens' monetary assemblies. And it almost disappeared when she discovered from Eve that there existed a multiplicity of community-based currencies alongside the central bank's. As Eve explained, any group who wanted to create its own currency was given the digital tools and entitled to do so, and a small fee was charged whenever someone wanted to convert it into the national currency. As a result, from northern California to Kosti's native Crete, local authorities had issued digital currencies for transactions within their communities using a model very similar to Jerome, their advantage being that they kept value produced locally within the community. Unlike in Our Now, where value produced in Aberdeen can freely emigrate to London, in the Other Now any transfer of wealth could be regulated by increasing or decreasing the amount charged for exchanging local for national currency, in proportion to the imbalance of wealth and trade flows between the two cities.

Impressed by these local innovations, Eva was eager to learn how things worked on a global scale. If such a system regulated imbalances between Aberdeen and London, were similar systems in place to lessen imbalances, not to mention injustices, in the trade between, say, Britain and Botswana? In reply, Eve described what Eva considered the most intriguing feature of the Other Now's international monetary system.

Trade

As an employee of the International Monetary Project, or IMP, the successor to the IMF, Eve was perfectly placed to answer Eva's questions. The first surprise for her was Eve's denunciation of the IMF before it turned into the IMP in 2013. 'Our job at the IMP,' Eve declared, 'is to do exactly the opposite of what the IMF used to do.'

The IMF is, indeed, notorious in Our Now. Since the 1970s, it has loaned money to bankrupt countries on terms that are the equivalent of debt bondage for their citizenry. Typically, when a country in Africa, Latin America or more recently Europe could no longer repay its government debts to foreign bankers, the IMF would step in to loan the money on neo-colonial conditions: wholesale transfer of public property to the international oligarchy, school and hospital closures, cuts in pensions and wages below the poverty line for the majority. Wherever the IMF visited, it left behind a black hole filled with pain.

By contrast, according to Eve, the IMP was not in the business of lending money. With private bankers gone, the world had no use for a cruel international bailiff, which is what the IMF had turned into; the IMP's remit was on the one hand to stabilize the world economy, and on the other to invest money directly in the regions of the world that needed it to develop, but without indebting them.

'You mean to tell me that the socialists have finally invented the magic money tree of their dreams?' Eva asked.

Unfazed, Eve reminded her alter ego of that which they both knew intimately: the magic money tree had been invented decades before by bankers like their ex-employer Lehman. No, Eve explained, the IMP imposed a couple of levies upon net exporters of goods and money that helped stabilize world trade and global money flows. And the proceeds from these levies were then channelled as free development funds to the world's least advantaged regions.

For decades, some countries in Our Now have been net exporters, while others have been net importers. For example, Germany has always exported far more to Greece and many other countries than it imports from those countries. For Germany, this is known as a trade surplus, the mirror image of Greece's trade deficit. This is a very common situation, even between rich countries. For example, Britain has been in a persistent trade deficit with Germany, indeed the rest of the world, since the Second World War, as has the United States. Since the 1960s America has bought more stuff from Germany, Japan and, increasingly, from China than it has exported to these countries. The problem arises when these persistent trade imbalances grow and grow and grow.

The reason that expanding trade imbalances reliably lead to trouble is that to pay for, say, German car imports, a deficit country such as Greece must ultimately borrow more and more from the surplus country in order to afford them. The same goes for the United States: having run trade deficits with Japan, Europe and China for decades, the only way it has been able to maintain its superpower status is by ratcheting up its reliance on Wall Street to attract money from Chinese banks, Japanese capitalists and European oligarchs. Borrowing constantly from Peter to pay Paul is an ill-advised strategy, but borrowing from Peter to pay Peter is more foolish still, as the deficit countries spiral into ever greater indebtedness and deepening reliance on chronically unreliable bankers.

The problem gets worse when the loans used to pay for a country's net imports are in a currency that the country does not issue. For example, Argentina, which has the peso as its currency, finds it impossible to borrow in pesos from American banks to import, say, oil because of the fear that the peso will devalue, in which case the American bank will lose money. So Argentina is forced to borrow in dollars, despite the fact that the Argentinian central bank can only print pesos. Similarly, Greece uses the euro, a currency that it cannot issue.

The moment American bankers stop lending dollars to Argentina, the country is unable to refinance its mountain of dollar debt. Again, Greece is similar. Even though it has the same currency as Germany, the euro, the chronic Greek trade deficit with Germany translates into a constant flow of loaned euros from Germany to Greece so that the Greeks can keep buying more and more German goods. The slightest interruption in the flow of new loans from the surplus country to the deficit country causes the whole house of cards to collapse. This is when the IMF steps in. Its personnel fly into Buenos Aires or Athens, take black limousines to the finance minister's office and state their terms: we shall lend you the missing dollars or euros on condition that you impoverish your people and sell the family silver to our mates, the oligarchs of this country and the world. Or words to that effect.

That's when TV screens fill with images of angry, and often hungry, demonstrators in Buenos Aires or Athens. Time and again history has shown that the periodic economic recessions that result from trade imbalances poison the deficit country's democracy, incite contempt for its people in the surplus country, which then prompts xenophobia in the deficit country. Simply put, sustained trade deficits – and surpluses, their mirror image – never end well.

How does the IMP prevent this tragedy in the Other Now? Eve was pleased to explain. For starters, the IMP issued a new digital currency called the Kosmos. This was decided at the IMP's inaugural congress in 2015 in Mumbai. There it was agreed that the Kosmos would never be printed, nor used for actual transactions between persons or companies, but used exclusively for accounting purposes by states and trading blocks. People on the streets of London or Birmingham would still transact among themselves in pounds, Americans deal in dollars, the Japanese in yen. Similarly, no one would notice a difference when they travelled or imported goods. Britons travelling to China or buying a computer from Japan would still need renminbi and yen.

The great innovation was that all trade between countries or blocks affiliated to the IMP is denominated in Kosmos, or Ks for short. When, for example, a German car crosses the Atlantic to be sold in America, the buyer pays in dollars and the German manufacturer receives euros. Except that, in between, the dollars are first converted into Ks before then being converted again into euros. The IMP, which keeps a ledger of all transactions, then adds that sum of Ks simultaneously to the United States' tally of total imports and to Germany's tally of total exports. Periodically, the IMP penalizes countries in proportion to their trade deficit or surplus. For example, if the US–German trade becomes grossly skewed, both Germany and the United States are charged the Trade Imbalance Levy. This works simply and automatically: a certain number of Ks are withheld from the German central bank's account at the IMP in proportion to Germany's trade surplus with the United States. And an equivalent number of Ks is withheld from the United States' account at the IMP in proportion to America's trade deficit with Germany.

Eva wanted to know what the IMP does with these Ks that it withholds.

'They flow into a common fund called the International Redistribution and Development Depository,' Eve explained, 'which uses them to fund green investments, especially in public health, education, renewable energy grids, transport systems and organic agriculture. Most of them go to the less developed regions in the world, which may include parts of the United States or, indeed, Germany – regions with low levels of domestic savings. Additionally, the IRDD funds migration flows in association with the Human Movement Project, where my partner Ebo works. What makes these monies so effective is that they are not loans but transfers.

'To avoid paying this levy,' Eve continued, 'a country needs to export more or less the same Kosmos value of goods and services as it imports. Initially, it was decided that the levy should be fixed at 5 per cent of deficits and surpluses before rising to 10 per cent by 2031. In practice, this means that, in the current year, 2025, any country that has a trade deficit of 100 billion Ks will have to pay 5 billion Ks, money that will go to the poorest humans and regions. Importantly, the exact same applies to a country running a surplus of 100 billion Ks.

'The beauty of the Trade Imbalance Levy is that it works well even when it fails. If by penalizing trade imbalances it succeeds in balancing trade flows, great. But even if it fails fully to eliminate trade imbalances, it generates funds that are then invested directly in underdeveloped regions via the IRDD. And that's not all.

'The key to world economic and political harmony,' Eve explained 'is the curtailment of all global imbalances – not just imbalances in the flow of goods and services but also in the flow of money from one economic block to another, from one country to another.'

It was at IMP's congress in Shanghai in 2021, she explained, that the IMP's Kosmos payment system was extended to prevent sudden influxes of speculative money into poorer

countries' economies. In Our Now, such invasions resemble a
plague of locusts. Every time Wall Street sniffs the opportunity
for a lucrative deal in a poor country – the discovery of an oil
field, a boom in house prices, a new crop of soya beans – they
flood the place with their easy money. Very quickly, that flood
inflates local house prices and the country's share market.
A semblance of enrichment leads local people to do stupid
things: they take out loans to get in on the money-making,
usually by investing in white elephants. Before long, the
bubble bursts. Always quicker to react and better informed,
Wall Street extracts its money swiftly at the first whiff of
danger, and the whole economy collapses.

To keep a check on these money invasions and subsequent
exoduses, the IMP instituted a second penalty: the Surge
Funding Levy. It is, very simply, a fee levied on monies wired
across borders that kicks in above a certain threshold and
increases in proportion to the speed and volume of these
transfers. Once triggered, the IMP withholds from any
transfer between, say, the United States and Brazil a number
of Ks in proportion to the scale of the surge. As in the case of
the Trade Imbalance Levy, the withheld Ks flow automatically
to the IRDD.

'In fact, by shifting wealth to the global south,' Eve added,
'these measures have given the governments of developing
countries the necessary latitude to agree to stricter emission
limits as part of our International Green New Deal.'

Eva's last question was a technical one: 'How is the
exchange rate between the IMP's Ks and all the national
currencies determined?'

'By me,' answered Eve, half-joking. Eve explained that
she worked in the IMP's Currency Auctions Directorate,

which held daily international auctions in order to work out appropriate exchange rates, so that the demand for each currency, expressed in Ks, matched almost exactly the quantity of that currency on offer from its central bank and private actors.

The IMP had, in summary, instituted a market-based, almost fully automated system of global discipline with the potential to balance out trade and money flows. Built into that system was a mechanism generating money that funded the transition of developing regions to low-carbon energy, green transport, organic agriculture, as well as decent public education and health systems. And all of it relied on the international agreement – first struck in Mumbai in 2015 and then extended in Shanghai in 2021 – that all trade and money flows should pass through the IMP's digital ledger and be denominated in Ks.

Eva had to admit she was much impressed.

Land

On 27 January 1967, the day three NASA astronauts died tragically in an Apollo launch test, the United States, the Soviet Union and Britain signed the Outer Space Treaty. It stipulated that everyone had the right to explore the moon and other celestial bodies but no one could take ownership of them or parts of them 'by claim of sovereignty, by means of use or occupation, or by any other means'. Ever since Eva had become aware of this obscure treaty, she had wished it applied also on earth.

A true liberal, Eva disdained monopoly. And to her mind there could be no greater monopoly than ownership of a piece of land. In this respect, she was in good company. Her favourite dead Englishman, J. S. Mill, once wrote that landlords 'grow richer, as it were in their sleep, without working, risking or economizing ... In what would they have been wronged,' Mill wondered, 'if society had, from the beginning, reserved the right of taxing the spontaneous increases of rent, to the highest amount required by financial exigencies?' Another hero of Eva's, the French economist Léon Walras, had gone further. He argued that land must be publicly owned and the accrued rents paid to the public as a social dividend, either in the form of money or public services.

So Eva was even more impressed to discover that Walras's idea had been adopted and written into law in the Other Now. In her dispatches Eve reported that, in a stunning reversal of the enclosures, which in eighteenth- and nineteenth-century England had privatized common land and sparked off capitalism, in the Other Now all land titles had been transferred to regional authorities. The UK's Great Ground Reform Act of 2017 established a ground commons authority for each county. Something similar transpired a year later in the United States, where Congress passed the Ground Trusts Act. On both sides of the Atlantic, every county's freehold titles were then transferred swiftly to its gComms, as the ground commons authorities or ground trusts came to be known. To appease the current owners of land, the acts included transitional arrangements granting existing private landlords life-long free leases. As for companies, the shift to one person one share one vote made it easier to strike agreements with the ground trusts on land use.

The basic idea, Eva gathered, was that each gComms divided its land between social zones and commercial zones, collecting rents from the commercial zones to finance social housing and space for social enterprises in its social zones. There were two types of commercial zone. One was land for housing, to be occupied by those able and willing to pay market prices. The other was commercial space for business. The key to the system was the Permanent Auction Subletting Scheme (PASS), a mechanism the OC rebels designed to ensure that communities could extract maximum rents from their commercial zones.

The essence of PASS was worryingly simple. Hosted within each gComms' website, PASS was a comprehensive listing of every building in its commercial zones. At the beginning of each year, anyone who occupied a building in a commercial zone, as a business or a resident, had to visit the PASS web page and next to the listing of the building they occupied put in what they believed to be the market value of the premises. PASS would then compute their monthly rent as a fixed portion of that self-declared market value. No audits. No red tape. No haggling with gComms regarding the level of the rent or of the 'true' market value of the space.

What stopped those using land in a commercial zone from undervaluing their premises? The answer lay in another feature of PASS: a virtual bidding room where any visitor to the website could bid for any building – any office or shop, any house or flat – within a commercial zone. Anyone offering to pay a higher annual rent for a property than its existing occupier had the right to take it over – after an appropriate transition period, which varied in length according to the type of building and the circumstances of the occupants. This permanent auction kept occupants honest. Set the value of the land or building you occupy too high and you pay too much rent. Set it too low and you risk eviction.

In PASS Eva recognized what academic economists refer to as a self-revelation mechanism design – arrangements that motivate people to act honestly, as in the famous method of dividing a pie between two people, whereby one cuts the pie and the other chooses which piece they want. When, later, Eva told Costa about PASS, he recognized it too, but from a somewhat different context.

'Sounds like a reverse antidosis,' he muttered.

Eva had to look the term up online. In ancient Athens, she discovered, the demos had decreed that rich citizens had a duty to pay for particular public services, the liturgies. The justification was the prevailing view that, since the city made private wealth possible, the demos that governed the city had the right to make such demands of the wealthy. Individuals that the assembly decreed should pay for, say, a play to be staged, had a choice: pay up or, if they believed they had been unfairly selected, file for antidosis.

Antidosis was a legal suit. When the assembly picked, say, Crito to pay for a play or a religious ceremony, he had the right to argue that, say, Phaedo should have been picked instead because in Crito's estimation Phaedo was better off. If Phaedo disagreed, he had the right to refuse but only if he was willing to accept that his whole estate would be given to Crito and that he would receive Crito's in return. Thus Crito was given pause before claiming Phaedo was richer, and Phaedo thought twice before he disagreed.

PASS was designed similarly, but in reverse: instead of acting as a safeguard for those who were unfairly declared wealthier than they were, it prevented an occupant of real estate from under-declaring its value and short-changing the community.

Eva's qualms and questions were legion. How were houses and land distributed in the social zones? Who got the nicer of the council-owned homes there? How did one move house? Above all, who ran the gComms? And yet, despite her concern that the whole system left too much room for authoritarian collectivism, Eva could not help but admire PASS: an automated, fully fledged market mechanism that, in the absence of private ownership, nonetheless revealed land's true value and contributed maximally to public projects under conditions of full transparency. A refreshing lack of bureaucracy, not to mention estate agents – all exciting features that she found hard to scoff at.

The next batch of dispatches answered some of Eva's questions, though not all of them to her satisfaction. A county-wide citizens' assembly, the County Association, oversaw the division of land between commercial and social zones, and then the division of commercial zones between business and residential uses, and the distribution of properties within the social zones. Once again, its members were selected randomly with the help of an algorithm that guaranteed fair representation of the various groups and communities living in the county.

Setting aside too much land for social zones meant less money to invest in them. On the other hand, expanding the commercial zones too much would leave too little room for social housing. Similarly, prioritizing business within the commercial zones at the expense of residential housing would limit the availability of property for wealthier residents whose higher spending capacities might draw successful corporations into the area and generally fuel the local economy. One of the hardest decisions the County Association faced was how much room to leave for newcomers: too much might antagonize the locals, too little would prevent new blood from enriching the local community.

As Eva had surmised, the most delicate of the County Association's tasks was the allocation of social housing in the absence of a price mechanism. Who qualified? And of those who qualified, who got the more desirable properties?

To create peace of mind in the community, Eve explained, tenure was guaranteed once you had been allocated a property within a social zone. But when someone chose to move out, or died, or a new property was built, the available property was allocated using a randomized digital raffle. Anyone wishing to move into the county and who put themselves forward was guaranteed a minimum probability of securing a property. This ensured that everyone had a decent chance. However, the odds of winning were set higher for applicants that interviewed well and rose in inverse proportion to the deposits in the candidate's PerCap Accumulation account – penalizing, in other words, those who could afford to bid for land or homes in the commercial zones.

The spectre of so much social control terrified Eva. She loved markets for one important reason: the freedom they granted from social obligations and power dynamics. To get something you just paid for it, anonymously, without having to befriend or negotiate, and certainly without having to convince some panel of strangers that you were sufficiently deserving. Nonetheless, Eva recognized that, when it came to land, capitalism denied most people that freedom.

What good is the freedom to buy a penthouse apartment in Kensington, she thought, *if you're broke and house prices are guaranteed to rise faster than your income, no matter how hard you work?*

If anything, the Other Now's use of permanent auctions in commercial zones and lotteries in social zones seemed to her far more liberal than the capitalist real estate markets she loved and despised in equal measure, for they provided a far better defence against monopoly.

'Could I be turning into a convert?' Eva scribbled in the margin of one of Eve's dispatches.

Borders

Over the last ten years, as other liberals were yielding to the 'pragmatism' of increasingly tougher immigration controls, Eva's spiritual loneliness had grown. Instinctively she opposed fences patrolled by armed guards, funded and empowered by some ethnocentric nation state. From 2016 onwards, she had been appalled by the surge in what she considered xenophobia among her political kin. So when she learned that Ebo, Eve's partner and Agnes's dad, led something called the Human Movement Project, she was eager to know more.

Under capitalism, globalization relied on the freedom of money and commodities to cross borders. Trillions of dollars circled the planet incessantly and at the speed of light. Countless container loads of goods crossed the great oceans and every boundary humanity had erected. And yet in so many places people were fenced in, enjoying none of the freedom afforded to toxic money, plastic toys or seasonal fruit. Scores of Mexicans gathered in the shadow of the US–Mexican border wall, weighing up the risk of scaling the barbed wire, while trucks laden with car parts, computers and beer passed freely onto US soil. Africans drowned in their thousands in the Mediterranean as they attempted to follow the vegetables their continent exported to Europe. In the name of refashioning the world as a borderless global village, globalization was building new fences and reinforcing older ones everywhere.

The Human Movement Project, Eve explained, had a simple remit: to facilitate freedom of movement for humans without inflaming further discontent within communities receiving newcomers. In his inaugural speech as HMP coordinator, her partner had pointed out that immigrants have always contributed net wealth to their destination countries – even under capitalism – but because the gains have been reaped disproportionately by the rich, the vast majority of the native population have enjoyed none of the benefits. All they see is greater competition for increasingly scarce social housing, amenities, health services and schools. For those in southern Europe, for example, forced to wave goodbye to their children as they set off in search of decent wages and dignity elsewhere, the arrival of migrants only intensifies their bitterness and their desire to claim something for themselves.

'You are right to want your country back,' Ebo had said in his speech. 'You are right to want to take back control. But first you must first take control of your community.'

Ebo and many other OC rebels were convinced that empowering people and giving them a greater sense of social status and agency was key to unlocking their readiness to appreciate the benefits of immigration. The gComms and the County Associations were the primary means by which they achieved this at the regional level. The Citizens' Juries that held corporations to account were another substantial source of grass-roots authority. The demise of shareholding, meanwhile, dramatically reduced inequality, while Dividend and Legacy accounts wiped the worry lines from people's faces. These were the foundation, Ebo had argued, for widespread support for a liberal migration policy.

But immigration policy itself needed radical change too. One such change was to devolve the power to grant visas to the regional gComms. Instead of the state deciding how many visas to issue and to whom, it was now down to the County Associations to consider visa requests directly from potential migrants. Additional funds for new homes and amenities would be allocated by the Human Movement Project and the International Monetary Project's IRDD to those counties who chose to grant migrant visas. If they did, the potential migrants would simply be entered into the same lottery for space in the social zones as any incomer, with their odds adjusted according to their performance in remote interviews conducted by a panel of randomly chosen residents.

'Global solidarity manifesting itself at local level,' was how Eve described it.

'Is it any wonder they never had to deal with Brexit or Trump?' wrote Iris in her diary.

Digital renaissance

In 2020, when Covid-19 hit and unemployment abruptly swelled, Eva had noticed a puzzling piece of graffiti on a wall near their local pub in Brighton: IF YOU HAVE NO JOB YOU HAVE NO LEISURE. At the time she took it to mean simply that without decently paid work, every waking minute becomes a struggle and it is impossible ever to rest; leisure and work become indistinguishable. Five years later, she found herself reminded of this graffiti as she read Eve's account of the Other Now's digital economy and began to see the assertion in a rather different light.

Initially, Eva had considered the harvesting of data by Facebook, Google and others for the purposes of advertising a pretty innocuous way for consenting adults to trade a little bit of privacy for some rather desirable free leisure services. But as Costa would point out whenever given half a chance, Facebook and Google, Twitter and Instagram, Amazon and the rest were not mere service providers. Nor were their profits rewards for services rendered. No, they were gigantic behaviour modification machines, addicting and provoking, teasing and enraging their users in order to maximize engagement and the profiling data – and profits – that came with it.

'Big tech only enables two people to communicate if it can manipulate their behaviour,' Costa would insist on the rare occasions that he and Eva had argued the matter.

This was what he meant when he said that social media was proletarianizing us all. Facebook's users provided both the labour that went into the machine and the product that was sold by it.

'Even Walmart, a company renowned for its capacity to squeeze every drop of value out of its workers, pays out 40 per cent of its total revenue in wages,' Costa would complain. 'But Facebook pays only 1 per cent of its revenues to its employees and precisely nothing to its users!'

That was back in 2019. By 2025, Eva had become convinced that no self-respecting liberal could condone big tech's mass manipulation techniques nor defend its gains as a fair reward for entrepreneurship. Its returns were only made possible by a species of techno-feudalism that made billions of people work for it for free.

And so, when she read Eve's detailed description of the digital economy forged by the OC rebellion, Eva caught herself cheering. The tipping point was the double strike action against Facebook that took place on 5 November 2012. Like the earlier Day of Inaction against Amazon, the Face the Music strike involved a boycott by Facebook's users, but this time they struck not as customers but as unpaid data labourers, striking in solidarity with Facebook's actual employees, by simply not visiting their Facebook pages. In conjunction with the new corpo-syndicalist legislation which shrank and eventually eliminated the share markets – doing away with those perpetually loss-making powerhouses, like Netflix and Uber, that grew on the back of speculation rather than profit – the wave of tech strikes left the major data-harvesting businesses in turmoil. The killer blow, however, came from the various Digital Rights Acts, which granted full property rights to every person on earth over their personal data.

This transformed the Internet economy overnight, driving the behaviour manipulation machines to extinction and fostering in their place a diverse ecosystem of countless digital businesses with many of the characteristics of consumer associations. Starved of their targeted advertising revenues and access to stock exchanges, the new shareholders of Google, Facebook and their ilk – employees owning one share each – were forced to seek the financial support of their community of users. In a surprisingly short time, what used to be the world's greatest and greediest private monopolies had mutated into vast digital communes.

The key to the Digital Renaissance, as Eve called it, was the micropay platform that the OC rebels cheekily named Penny For Your Thought. In operational terms, it combined Netflix's subscription model with the British National Health Service's principle of universal provision.

App developers needing people's data had to pay to get it from consenting users, who could choose which parts of their data to sell and to whom. At the same time, anyone using an app had to pay the developer for access to it. The sums involved were extremely small for the individual, but for an app with vast pools of users they could add up to large amounts. More importantly, the amount any individual received in micropayments went a long way towards covering the cost of their Internet usage. But if any user or developer was unable to pay the stream of micropayments demanded by Penny For Your Thought, they could apply for their PerCap Legacy account to be charged directly. No one was denied access to anonymized data or desirable apps, even while no digital service or data was provided for free.

Free now from the predation of the tech giants, millions of small tech corporations emerged, and a rowdy digital marketplace was born that could never have flourished under Our Now's techno-feudalism.

'Penny For Your Thought made the era of targeted advertising, based on "free" digital services look like a digital Middle Ages,' Eve commented.

The only potential drawback of this vibrant new ecology was that it lacked the sheer scale of the tech giants which had made their data so potent. Without access to a pool of data on an equivalent scale, many technologies – including life-saving diagnostic tools, for example – would remain out of reach. In Our Now in 2019, for example, Google had collaborated with Britain's National Health Service. In return for access to the NHS's vast pool of patient data, it had been able to develop a machine-learning app capable of diagnosing a dangerous eye malady as effectively as the best ophthalmologists. But the contract stipulated that, after a few years, the NHS would have to buy the app from Google like any other commercial user. Google was eating its cake and having it too. Keen to press machine learning into public service on terms that reflected the actual value of people's data, the OC rebels created a glorious new institution: the Sovereign Data Fund, an ingenious means of extracting value from that data before returning it to the community.

Eve explained that all data, both public and private, was stored anonymously on the Sovereign Data Fund's cloud computer network. Companies wishing to use it as Google had used the NHS data had to pay a royalty into that country's fund in return for a licence to use it. The more successful the technology, the more royalties the fund accrued, thus funding further technological breakthroughs.

Once more, it seemed to Eva, leisure and work were becoming hard to distinguish. Only in the Other Now the sense of alienation that lay behind that Brighton graffiti had been replaced with something different, something more like its opposite: empowerment.

Grossly demoted GDP

It counts special locks for our doors and the jails for the people who break them ... It counts napalm and nuclear warheads and armoured cars for the police to fight the riots in our cities ... Yet [it] does not allow

for the health of our children, the quality of their
education or the joy of their play. It does not include
the beauty of our poetry ... It measures everything, in
short, except that which makes life worthwhile.

Bobby Kennedy's famous condemnation of GDP, the dollar
metric of a nation's total income, had always irritated Eva
despite its obvious poetic quality – or perhaps because of it.
During her time as a postgrad in economics at the end of the
noughties, GDP-bashing had become something of a cottage
industry, although Eva had thought it was akin to lambasting a
maritime navigation device for failing to appreciate the beauty
of the ocean and its impact on the human psyche.

'Of course GDP rises when a terrible earthquake kills
thousands,' she would assert to the students in her seminars.
'That's what it's meant to do: count the monetary expense of
the rescue efforts at first and the cost of rebuilding later. And of
course its needle does not move when a lover's gesture uplifts
one's soul or a bush fire consumes a forest. The point of GDP
is not to condone the earthquake or to make us indifferent to
intangible beauty or environmental disaster. It is to measure
that which it was designed to measure: money expenditures
by some that add, equivalently, to the incomes of others.'

Monetary profit drives capitalism. Under capitalism, like
it or not, society's resources are attracted by the anticipation
of higher profit and repelled by anything that reduces the
bottom line. Eva's view was that GDP is a snapshot of these
forces at work – a highly effective one that does not purport
to be anything more or less. 'It seeks to capture capitalism's
dynamic and to map out the types of endeavour that generate
money – "the alienated essence of our life", as I believe your

beloved Karl Marx once put it. To dump GDP and replace it with an arbitrary measure of something … nicer would be to take our finger off capitalism's pulse – to ditch our only means of gauging the beast's behaviour.'

Every time an environmentalist demanded a new, cuddlier metric with which to replace GDP, Eva despaired. 'If we want to protect trees or lakes that have no market price,' she argued, 'we should just do it: slap preservation orders on them! What's the point of concocting an arbitrary price substitute by which to measure their intangible value?'

The irony is, Eva had thought to herself, *these hip anti-capitalists are their own worst enemy*. Under capitalism, the only way a tree or a lake can be assigned a quantifiable value is by putting it up for sale to see what price it fetches. In the absence of any alternative to capitalism, Eva used to tell her students, we need to stop criticizing GDP and instead invest in immeasurable public goods like the health of our children or the beauty of their poetry.

At least, that was Eva's view when, like almost everyone else, she believed there really was no alternative to capitalism. In the light of Eve's latest dispatches, she was starting to wonder.

On the one hand, markets in the Other Now appeared to be in rude health despite, or maybe because of, capitalism's demise; a great deal of economic activity in Kosti and Eve's society could still be measured in terms of monetary incomes. On the other hand, a lot of private-sector activity was driven neither by net revenue maximization nor by market forces but by instruments such as the Socialworthiness Index, which played a large role in diverting resources to various activities. Compiled by customers, neighbours, artists and the community at large, the index assigned a number to an economic activity that reflected neither price nor the quantity supplied. Or take the Citizens' Juries' power to dissolve enterprises for failing the public interest. These both created strong incentives for corporations to diverge from business plans that maximized profits. Freed from the tyranny of their share prices and the fear of hostile takeovers, corporations were more alive to society's needs. So too with the County Associations, whose members allocated land for the benefit of local communities. While they exploited market forces to generate funding for social purposes, their decisions were uninfluenced by the prices generated by capitalist real estate markets.

Once capitalism had died, and markets were freed from private ownership, a different kind of value took over. Instead of judging something's worth by its exchange value – what it would fetch in return for something else – the Other Now judged worth according to experiential value – the benefit the thing brought to the person who used it. Prices, quantities and monetary profits were no longer the sole masters of society. And the more experiential value liberated itself from the hegemony of exchange value, the less meaningful or relevant GDP would be. And so it was in the Other Now, Eve confirmed. Although it continued to play a role in measuring monetary incomes, GDP was simply one of many metrics used to monitor the economy – a demotion that would have made no sense before capitalism died.

To the market's rescue?

Markets fail all the time. Eva knew this as well as the next woman. But until very recently her faith in markets had never failed. She would not allow it to fail because she could not conceive of an alternative way of allocating scarce resources that worked consistently better and, more importantly, did not empower some central authority to make decisions about who gets what.

In the 1920s and 1930s, her liberal forebears had assailed socialists who aspired to replace markets with some centrally designed system for allocating raw materials, jobs and goods with a powerful critique: no human mind or organization, however smart and well meaning, can ever know what society wants, what capacities it has or how it should use its resources. It was not, the free-market liberals maintained, a question of insufficient computing capacity. In the same way that squaring the circle is not just immensely hard but absolutely impossible, working out what we *all* want, and how we should get it, is downright undoable. Only by groping around in the marketplace as individual consumers and producers can we hope to find out what each of us wants and what each is capable of. At least, that was their story.

Eva believed it. But then, one day in 2019, her faith was tested. Browsing the Amazon website, scrolling through the list of books it was recommending to her, she realized that its algorithm was spookily accurate at guessing her preferences. Experimenting, she turned her attention to music. The big tech companies had all sussed her out. Amazon, Spotify and Apple Music all picked songs she liked and some she was interested in trying out. She needed only to type a character or two into Google Search, and it completed her words. Netflix, meanwhile, inundated her with movie suggestions that only a friend who knew her film tastes inside out would have made. Though it might not be perfect, it was no longer true, she suddenly realized, that a centrally designed system could never know what we want.

With liberal arguments against communism's inherent inefficiency disproved by capitalism's technologies, Eva's faith in capitalism now hung by a single thread: her belief that a centrally planned system, even if potentially efficient, posed a grave threat to human rights and personal freedom. But was this enough? Capitalism triumphed in 1991 not so much because the citizens of the USSR or East Germany lacked freedom but because of the queues they had to endure to get hold of anything, whether a loaf of bread or a TV set. Had it been solely a question of freedom, Eva feared, the red flag would still be flying over the Kremlin – perhaps over the White House too.

Once big tech had given the lie to the liberals' insistence that individual preferences could never be centrally served, Eva concluded that Silicon Valley's greatest, and perhaps only, beneficiary was the Chinese Communist Party. She saw no reason why Beijing could not, in time and with development, adopt the very same technologies that allow Alibaba – China's equivalent of Amazon – to predict accurately what its customers will want next in order to manage the country's entire economy. It already had the authority to do so; all it needed was the means. And once artificial intelligence advanced a little more, what would there be to stop Chinese-style communism from overrunning markets completely?

Such concerns were already troubling Eva by the time she found herself in Costa's San Francisco lab in 2025. Indeed, they were responsible for her openness to the Other Now dispatches, which surprised even her. Normally, she would have railed against the society they described. The OC rebels had banned share markets, abolished labour markets and banished banking. They had taken land into public ownership and denied big tech the very oxygen it breathed. So why did Eva, the archetypal liberal, see in the Other Now, which was in so many respects a liberal's nightmare, a glorious opportunity for markets?

The reason was that the Other Now was brimming with features that any liberal would find hard to resist: an absence of income and sales taxes; the freedom of workers to move from company to company while taking their personal capital with them; the curtailment of large companies' market power; universal freedom from poverty, but also from a welfare state demanding that benefit-recipients surrender their dignity at the door of some social security office; a payments system that was free, efficient and which did not empower the few to print money at the expense of the many; a permanent auction for commercial land that exploited market forces to the full in the interests of social housing; an international monetary system that stabilized trade and the flow of money across borders; a welcoming attitude to migrants based on empowering local communities and helping them absorb newcomers.

Yes, almost everything Eve told her made her uneasy, but it also pointed to a world in which markets at last fulfilled their proper purpose. With private property, corporate empires and turbocharged finance all gone, the OC rebels had found it possible, and desirable, to construct markets that were genuinely competitive – the kind of markets that a true liberal could only dream of under capitalism.

Eva went over Eve's dispatches, scouring the Other Now for evidence to the contrary, but by the time she had combed them for a third time, the absurd idea was firmly planted in her mind: a proper market revival requires the end of capitalism.

By now Eva and Iris had been staying with Costa for two months. Eva had applied for study leave from Sussex University to prolong her stay beyond the end of the summer break. While her official excuse was that Thomas had promised to join her in November, Costa and Iris knew that her actual main reason was fascination with the Other Now. Both she and Iris had long since abandoned any doubt that it was real.

But while Eva's interest in the alternative present only grew, Costa's had been moving in the opposite direction. Kosti's dispatches to him had for a long while been generating diminishing returns. By the end of September, his communications with Kosti were confined to technical exchanges for the maintenance of the wormhole. In fact, as Eva and Iris had been corresponding with their alternative selves, Costa and Kosti had been struggling to keep the wormhole stable. Strict rationing of the data that passed through it was now vital if they were to avoid its collapse. According to Costa's records, Eva had proved by far the keener correspondent, with Iris taking time to reflect between messages. By the end of October, Eva had used up almost all her entire quota of data, while Iris was not even halfway through hers.

Eva had just received a dispatch from Eve that referred tantalizingly to the 'deep monetary Crunch of 2022', when Costa told her that her time was up. Eva was torn. On the one hand, she was angry and frustrated that Eve had not mentioned this event before; on the other, she was strangely relieved at the revelation that the Other Now was not immune to crisis. She pleaded with Costa for additional kilobytes, but he was adamant: 'You have the equivalent of a short paragraph,' he told her. So Eva turned to Iris and tried to impress upon her the importance of using some of her quota to find out about the Crunch that Eve had referred to. For Eva wanted to use her last missive to Eve to ask something else.

'How is Agnes dealing with adolescence?' she enquired.

'She finds me fairly intolerable,' Eve replied. 'Ebo less so. But overall, she seems pretty happy and fulfilled.'

Eva was oddly comforted. Anxious about her reunion with Thomas after a difficult few years, she allowed herself to think that maybe his uphill struggle in life was neither inevitable nor, on a self-centred note, down to her DNA.

7

Trouble in Paradise

A hard-to-kill cockroach

By the time Eva began badgering Iris to find out about the Crunch of 2022, Iris's exchanges with Siris had taken her in a completely different direction – one in which markets, prices and incomes seemed distant, immaterial, tedious.

They had not got off to a good start. Heeding Costa's advice, as Eva had also done, Iris introduced herself to her counterpart with an autobiographical detail that no one else could have known: an incident that had taken place in 1974 during a raucous forty-eight-hour party at the country home of the sweet aristocrat who was later to secure her financial independence with a surprising bequest.

For half a century Iris had wanted to believe that the bequest was unconnected to that incident, rather than a silent apology for leaving her unprotected. To avoid reliving the violence and excruciating panic she had endured that weekend, she had suppressed the memory. Why had she retrieved it now? Convincing Siris of her identity was not the whole reason. Writing that first message, Iris was finally addressing an old, pent-up need. But Siris's angry response made her feel foolish and confirmed the depth of a pain that endured even more in the Other Now.

Gradually, however, the awkwardness dissipated as they discovered that, despite their eighteen-year separation and wildly different experiences, they were equally weighed down by the permanent spectre of male violence. To Iris's disappointment, though not surprise, Siris confirmed that the OC revolution had not made much of a difference in this particular regard. Corporations had been democratized, citizens' assemblies had sprung up, bankers and estate agents no longer existed, but structurally and psychologically – even in the most progressive circles – the relationship between women and men remained a zero-sum game, one that its historic winners continued to dominate.

'Mountains move, banking becomes extinct, even capitalism dies,' Siris wrote, 'but patriarchy lives on like a hard-to-kill cockroach. The difference is that it is now disguised beneath an even thicker veneer of political correctness.'

Siris's heated dispatches left Iris troubled. On the one hand, had she been told that the OC rebellion had killed off patriarchy, she would have dismissed the Other Now as an unsophisticated hoax. It was completely implausible to her that patriarchy would wither as a result of some political revolution, however transformative it might be in every other respect. Nonetheless, the intensity of Siris's fury at the Other Now's combination of political correctness and unyielding patriarchy took her aback – even while it put a smile on her face: for the first time in her life, she found herself on the receiving end of what her friends had been enduring for years.

The correspondence with Siris reaffirmed Iris's conviction that any utopia imagined by minds formed in a patriarchal world – however well meaning and progressive those minds might be – was bound to be a bleak place for women. It was a conviction she had held since she was fourteen years old, when her paternal grandmother, Anna, a brave figure who had agitated for women's lib when it was unfashionable and stigmatizing to do so, had urged Iris to imagine herself a suffragette too.

'Imagine, Iris,' she had said, 'that there was no state, no laws, no institutions of authority like the BBC or the Bank of England, no Royal Opera House or Football Association.'

The young Iris had tried in vain to comply.

'Now imagine also,' Anna continued, 'that we could all, women as well as men, have the chance to sit nicely around a large table, as equals, to discuss over many cups of tea the rules we want to work and play by, the institutions we need, the best form of governing our country, our community, our family affairs. Finally, imagine that this grand assembly succeeded in agreeing unanimously on what laws and institutions to put in place. Would that not be the good society? Isn't it fascinating to try to imagine what that society might be like?'

It was the disarming glow of excitement on her grandmother's sweet face that caused Iris to restrain herself. But Anna sensed Iris's intense scepticism and insisted she explain its source. Eventually, Iris came clean.

'Women would not be sitting at the table, Gran,' she asserted with her usual terrifying confidence. 'They would be standing, fretting, fetching drinks and food for the pontificating males, who would of course decide everything.'

In truth, it was not just the likelihood of men and women debating matters of state and power as equals that Iris doubted, but it was not until she was a first-year undergraduate that she was able to articulate precisely why she had rejected Anna's thought experiment so vehemently. As a student, she learned of Marx's contempt for the idea that the bourgeoisie would ever deliberate as equals with factory workers. Lesser minds would have seen Marx's objection as equivalent to her own: simply replace the working men with women. Not Iris. Despite their obvious similarity, she was adamant the hypotheses were not equivalent.

As a budding anthropologist, Iris had observed that, contrary to Marx's belief, men of different class backgrounds could, and often did, find common ground. By the 1960s, it was not uncommon for working men to be invited into chambers of commerce and boardrooms – even to Whitehall and Downing Street. How come? Conventional wisdom had it that, once workers were organized in effective trade unions, bosses had an interest in co-opting their leaders so as to establish industrial peace and strike mutually advantageous agreements.

Iris dismissed this explanation as unacceptably incomplete. Humanity's tragedy, she argued, was that common interests do not guarantee cooperation, even when the stakes are sky high. Something else is needed to bring people together first. A bond of trust and allegiance. Some sort of shared identity. What identity was it that the members of these conflicting social classes shared? What did they have in common as people that allowed them to establish common ground on wages and working conditions, on legislation and matters of state? Iris's answer caused much consternation among both the men and the women who heard it: it was their shared entitlement as men to use women.

'Behind every successful man is a surprised woman,' Iris liked to joke. 'And behind every successful deal between men from across the class divide there is a sexual contract that gives them joint, though unequal, ownership over women's labour – often over their bodies.'

Bosses had their trophy wives and an army of secretaries, administrators and support staff, while the male workers they routinely exploited had an even more exploited and downtrodden unpaid domestic labourer to return home to.

'It may not be much,' I remember Iris saying to me once, 'but it is just enough. After all, plenty of people with a 90 per cent mortgage are convinced they own their own homes. So it's hardly surprising that ownership of their wives' labour is enough to convince working-class men they have something in common with their bosses.'

War on love

Most women were aghast when Iris shared her conviction that an unspoken contract of female enslavement underpinned even the most progressive social pact. Her women friends, proud of feminism's advances, were angered when Iris casually dismissed its achievements. While she acknowledged that feminism had succeeded partially, in that millions of women had escaped servitude by claiming positions of authority – Maggie Thatcher being the prime example – they had only managed to do so by becoming honorary males. And only if they first found some other, usually browner, woman to take their place on the domestic front as a marginalized proletarian.

Iris's audacious theory was that, since at least the French Revolution, every time progressive movements scored a victory, women were pushed ever so slightly deeper into collective bondage, even while individual women flourished. Every time the franchise was extended to include men of smaller means and lower rank, women had paid the price by sinking even lower down the pecking order. So in the 1970s,

when most progressives thought women's place in society was
gradually improving, Iris saw a steady deterioration.

And when in the 1980s her friends were celebrating sexual
liberation and women's empowerment, Iris's analysis turned
gloomier still. Good sex was being reimagined, in her view,
as but another species of fair trade, while working men, their
fortunes waning in proportion to deindustrialization, looked
to sex to regain the power they felt rapidly slipping through
their fingers. Transactional sex was, of course, better than
sex under duress. But it did nothing to enrich, empower or
liberate women – or indeed men. Only a readiness to fall in
love could do that, because falling in love was, in her opinion,
the exact opposite of free-market, transactional sex.

'Falling in love is one the greatest acts of resistance against
Thatcherism's oeuvre!' she would declare. 'In an era when being
in control – of one's stocks, inventories, workers, timetable
– is valued above all else, falling in love means surrendering
control to an "other". It threatens the foundational ideology –
of exchange value, of individual agency and self-determination
– of financialized capitalism.

'Attaining happiness purely through joyous intimacy,
without paying for anything?' she said, adopting the deep
voice and angry tone of a captain of industry. 'Surrendering
unconditionally to another person, expecting nothing in
return and becoming genuinely fulfilled in doing so? It is so
damned anti-capitalist, so subversive an idea, such a threat
to our way of life that if the government had any sense they
would immediately start a War on Love as fierce as the War
on Drugs.'

By the late 1980s, of course, Thatcher had succeeded: the
idea that something could be given away for the joy of it was

almost unfathomable, and Iris identified an equivalent triumph in the arena of sexual politics. The young were being groomed into seeing sexuality as naturally selfish and exploitative. It became uncool to admit you had fallen in love. Girls were expected to look sexy all the time but were still scorned when they had sex, indoctrinated with the monopolist's mindset that to maximize profit they had to restrict supply. And all the while, the same people who were increasingly incapable of conceiving of a sexual dynamic other than he-takes-she-gives adopted a politically correct language of sexual equality entirely at odds with their own thinking and behaviour.

'Thatcherism robbed sex of its sexiness,' Iris once told me, 'turning it into a form of mutual masturbation, tinged with the ever-present threat of violence.'

This was soon after the Iron Lady's third election victory in 1987, shortly before Iris retreated permanently into her Brighton cocoon.

Love and death after capitalism

As a teenager, Iris had liked to imagine that the demise of capitalism would be a triumph for love, justice and, by extension, women's emancipation. By the late 1970s, that faith had faded. Now Siris's dispatches confirmed her fears.

In the early years of the OC rebellion, romance staged a comeback. As in all revolutions, great acts of courage led to great ruptures that yielded great love affairs. Admittedly, many of those relations burned bright but fast and fizzled out. Nevertheless, even as late as 2013, the OC revolution's most famous daughter, Esmeralda, issued a provocative call for the revolution's values 'to penetrate our sexual relations'

in a historic speech that came to be known as her Soho
Address.

> When I am having sex, I demand to be both an object
> and a subject.
>
> Just as I refuse to be either a waged worker or a
> capitalist employer, I refuse to be either a feminized
> object or a male subject.
>
> Just as I laugh at those who tell me I must only give
> myself to someone with whom I have a future, I laugh
> when people say 'It was just sex'. I refuse to endorse
> the belittlement of sex in the same way that I refuse to
> endorse its elevation onto some divine pedestal.
>
> Is it not time that we rejected all these false
> oppositions – sex versus love, subject versus object?
>
> At last we have done away with the oppressive belief
> that sex is everything, but must we now replace it with
> the alienating conviction that it means nothing?
>
> Is it not time to give up on defining sex? To realize
> that it has to do with everything at once: bodily joy,
> love, playfulness, but also with power?
>
> Our revolution challenged possessive individualism
> in all its forms. Our new laws and participatory
> institutions have put an end to the private ownership
> of corporations, of land, of credit and money creation.
> We have succeeded in reuniting the economic with the
> political, the moral with the efficient, the functional
> with the fair.
>
> Having struggled so hard to realize our new social
> arrangements, would it not be a pity to allow sex to

remain as a form of market transaction, as a power relationship?

Remember how radically we dealt with market power? We did not simply bolster some competition authority. No, we got rid of the stock exchange and we legislated so that workers have one share each. We replaced the credit ratings of financiers with the socialworthiness indices of the community. Comrades, we must be equally bold and radical when it comes to sex.

Take the issue of consent. Will we continue to rely on legal structures and lawyers to define consent? Will we continue to look to the state to enforce it in our bedrooms and our lives? Or should we instead begin anew by looking inside ourselves, as critically as we have looked at our political and financial institutions in recent years?

Speaking personally, I demand the right to consent to sex and not to be touched without it. But I also acknowledge that without desire there is nothing I want to consent to. And I know in my bones that desire can't help itself. It screams. It beseeches. It begs. If I have to ask, my desire must be weak. And to be honest, comrades, if he has to ask, it's over for me before it begins.

To have sex with you, I must desire you. And I can only desire you because you desire me because I desire you because – in other words – our desires create and continuously reinforce one another, forming a relationship in which I am both subject and object, giver and recipient. Comrades, make no mistake: this is the opposite of reciprocity, the antithesis of a market exchange.

Think about it: sex cannot be good and thus truly consensual, if I am giving you something in order to take something back. It can only be good and thus truly consensual, if I do it because I can't help myself. It is only good if I have lost control and I am loving it. Good sex, authentically consensual sex, can never be contractual, with specified terms of exchange. Nor can it be governed by codes of fairness nor confined to certain types of relationship.

Like two mirrors facing one another, two lovers generate an infinite self-reflection. Whatever it is that they are giving one another can never be itemized or quantified.

Comrades, we staged our revolution to replace rivalry with cooperation in all walks of life. Sex is as unquantifiable as an experience as any that people share – whether they are writing a song or glimpsing a comet blaze through the night sky.

Our revolution ended the division of profit and wage so that people can do things together gainfully without exploitation. It ended the division of the political from the economic for the same reason. It brought community into our corporations and embedded corporations in our communities.

Let us now – consciously – exploit the opportunity we have created for ourselves to end the division between sex and love, between subject and object, between desire and consent.

We have nothing to lose and a whole universe of pleasure to gain.

Weeks after reading Esmeralda's Soho Address, phrases in it still brought tears to Iris's eyes, It was a reminder that every revolution has its Alexandra Kollontai and its Rosa Luxemburg – magnificent, tragic women determined to use the rare opportunity handed them by history to put a dent in women's subjugation, while at the same time promoting humanity's broader interests. Like theirs, Esmeralda's dreams were also dashed, not least, in Iris's view, because the majority of women proved unequal to the task.

Siris had sent the Soho Address through the wormhole not as evidence that the sexual revolution she had hoped for had succeeded but as a vision of the glorious path not taken. After the initial burst of radicalism, Siris explained that the Other Now's economic and political institutions began to produce significant levels of shared prosperity, and with it came a renewed social conservatism.

By 2020, political correctness dominated public discourse to the extent that the language Esmeralda had used in her address was considered inappropriate. A definition of consent was demanded, debated and enshrined in law. Indeed, everything in the Other Now from 2013 onwards that Siris described led Iris to conclude that the end of capitalism had failed to bring to an end the sexual contract on which capitalism had relied.

'Remember our campaigns back in the days of the Gay Liberation Front?' Siris asked Iris.

'Of course I remember,' she replied.

'We fought for liberation, not equality,' said Siris. 'I wouldn't have bothered getting out of bed – let alone demonstrating in the streets – for the right to share in the misery of some sexually repressed straight person.'

'How could I forget?' Iris replied.

'Our dream was to change society radically, not just to be accepted by it,' Siris went on, recounting in detail over the course of several dispatches the vision they had fought for so audaciously.

It became obvious to Iris that, in reliving those times with her, Siris was responding to a deep-rooted but unfulfilled need of some kind. Iris wondered what it was. Did Siris lack friends in the Other Now? Or was it something more sinister: did she perhaps feel unsafe even mentioning these ideas?

'What has gone wrong?' Iris thought to herself. 'What happened to those young lesbians' commitment to build a broad liberation movement involving feminist, trade union and black organizations? How did we allow a movement intent on emancipation to embrace joyless, oppressive political correctness and, in so doing, to quash the vibrant, indeterminate liberty we were fighting for? How did a vision of freedom degenerate into a pathetic equality narrative that, at its worst, has translated into little more than the commercialization of queerness and the right to have kitsch weddings?'

The more she thought about it, the more convinced Iris was that the stupendous resilience of the sexual contract – the source of the crippling alienation she had railed against for as long as she could remember – was the worst news to have come from the Other Now, eclipsing all the good it had achieved and imperilling her already shaky faith in humanity. Perhaps, Iris thought, it was indeed time to turn to some other failure instead, if only to distract her from such a painful realization.

And so it was that, after days of resisting them, Iris acceded to Eva's demands and wrote to Siris on a different subject.

'I gather that 2022 was a year of monetary crisis. Was it serious?'

Siris confirmed that it had been. She described briefly how the Other Now's payments systems had almost collapsed and how, for the first time since the OC rebellion, there had been shortages and demonstrations in the streets. There had even been organized hacking attacks that revived the spirit and methods of the OC rebellion.

'Yes, 2022 was an awful year,' Siris wrote, 'not least because it was the year we lost Esmeralda.'

'What do you mean "lost"? What happened?' Iris asked.

'She was stabbed to death as she was walking home one night,' Siris replied.

Shocked, Iris demanded more information, but there was little Siris could offer. The assailant was never caught, she explained, and his identity remained unknown. Siris explained that the scene was caught on a surveillance camera meant to trigger a rapid police response in cases of assault. But the police did not respond fast enough and, after the fact, using the surveillance camera imagery to identify him would have violated his property rights over his data – rights that were cast in stone in the Other Now's legal system.

Many believed the murder to have been motivated by anger at the Crunch. Having led the rebellion against capitalism's financial system, Esmeralda was in the eyes of the world the designer of the Other Now's payments system, which many blamed for the crisis. Others disagreed.

Iris was devastated by the news of Esmeralda's murder. The night she received it, she turned to her friends for comfort. Eva was preoccupied with her own troubles, her son Thomas to be precise, but Costa proved a good listener, even if it was clear to Iris he could not fully share her pain. After she had unburdened herself, Costa stared forlornly out of the window.

'In ancient times,' he said eventually, 'women were murdered for resisting the absolute authority of the men who owned them. Today's Antigones and Cassandras are stabbed by random men in dark alleys. I am not sure this constitutes progress.'

The Crunch of 2022

Iris mourned Esmeralda as she would her own sister. The little interest she'd had in the Crunch of 2022 evaporated when she learned of her death. So when Siris sent through a long dispatch that laid bare the details of the crisis, the manner in which it had infected the entire international economy, and the authorities' response to the disaster, Iris simply handed it over to Eva.

From the first paragraph, Eva was pleased to see that it was diligently written and as detailed as one could expect from a non-economist. Intriguingly, the problem had started in a familiar fashion. With the end of commercial banking, small community-based credit brokers had emerged offering to match savers with lenders, but as long as all transactions were carried out on Jerome, the central bank's free digital payments system, a crisis was theoretically impossible: even if some borrowers defaulted and some lenders lost money, the absence of bankers' loans and markets for debt prevented a systemic failure involving universal losses. But that changed when certain shady brokers managed to shift a significant number of transactions away from Jerome and onto a dark network invisible to the monetary authorities.

Siris explained what happened by describing the experience of a friend of hers, Joyce, who almost lost her entire PerCap savings in this way. One day Joyce had been approached online by one of these nefarious brokers, calling itself Delaware Community Credit Services. DCCS offered to match her with a borrower who would pay, for a five-year loan, more than twice the interest rate she could get from the central bank. Moreover, DCCS told her that all being well she wouldn't even have to transfer the money out of her PerCap account. All she had to do was sign a contract barring herself from using the lent funds and granting DCCS the right to instruct her to transfer them to any account they specified during the five years of the agreement. *What could go wrong?* Joyce thought. *They're not even bothering to remove the money from my account.* What she did not know was what DCCS was planning to do with the access she was granting them to her money.

Once a few million Joyces had signed up, DCCS and others owned the right to shift vast amounts of money to whomever they chose. They then approached the gComms – the ground commons authorities who oversaw the distribution of each county's land – that they knew were eager to invest in developing new commercial sites (with a view to funding social housing in their social zones) and offered them immediate and plentiful financing in exchange for a cut of the gComms' future earnings. Once these contracts were signed, granting them the right to collect on future monetary gains, DCCS had secured access to two kinds of other people's money: existing savings belonging to Joyce and others, and future, public land rents to be collected by the gComms.

Eva knew from her experience at Lehman that if you give financiers access to two different income streams, they quickly find a way to make money by combining them. Which was exactly what they did. DCCS wrote a contract that afforded its bearer the right to draw parts of Joyce's money and, at the same time, to trade in part of a gComms' future earnings. These contracts, called mixed credit rights (MCRs), were then put up for sale on an improvised digital trading platform of their design. While it had no legal standing, this trading platform was not banned by law either, possibly because no lawmaker had thought of it. When, later, some of its instigators were brought to justice, their dubious defence was 'That which is not illegal is ethical.' Eva smiled when she read that, reminiscent as it was of the heady days of 2008.

Access to Joyce's real money had now been boosted in value by the expectation of the gComms' future earnings, and so it sold for more than was required to pay Joyce the interest DCCS had promised her. Soon, MCRs were selling like hot cakes and companies like DCCS had an idea. *Why just sell the damn things? Why not also buy them to resell later once their price goes up even further?* As long as the MCRs could be sold tomorrow for more money, it made sense.

Within a year, a large percentage of people's PerCap savings had been shifted onto the improvised and unregulated trading platforms that DCCS and others had created. As money flooded into the local authorities via their gComms, the value of their local digital currencies went up. Demand for land in the areas doing particularly well increased, further boosting prices and inflaming the trade in MCRs. As land was developed faster, both in the commercial and social zones, the purchasing power of the community as a whole increased, and all sorts of local companies flourished. Everyone was a winner – just as long as land prices kept rising.

Reading Siris's dispatch, Eva experienced a painful sense of déjà vu and knew what was coming next. It was a random event – a flood somewhere, according to Siris – that pushed land prices down in south-east England. Several MCRs that had factored in large increases in those land values tanked overnight on the informal trading platform. A cascade of MCR failures took less than a day to crash the purchasing power of one community currency after another. Companies whose business was conducted primarily in those currencies went bust. To address their own liquidity problems, the shadowy credit brokers, DCCS included, immediately exercised their right to transfer monies from Joyce's and others' PerCap accounts, leaving many of them empty.

For Eva, the whole calamity was depressingly familiar. But what happened next was not. As soon as the authorities woke up to what was unfolding, they acted fast. Thankfully, the tools they needed to reverse the ruinous cascade were already in place. Central banks replenished the PerCap accounts of Joyce and anyone else who had been badly hit, restoring their purchasing power. They also added a little more to all accounts for good measure. By adjusting the overall quantity of money upwards in this way, they were able to lift the gloom and boost society's animal spirits.

Companies that had lost significant sales as a result of devaluations in their local currency received one-off cash injections too. And at an emergency conference the International Monetary Project decided to provide support to national currencies that had suffered disproportionately. Once the dust had settled, legislation was introduced that beefed up the citizens' monetary assemblies which regulated currencies, dismantled all informal credit trading platforms and banned contracts between savers and credit brokers of the sort that had created the bubble and put Joyce's savings in jeopardy.

By early 2022, the Crunch had been overcome. Human nature's capacity for mischief had proved itself to be irrepressible once more, but the Other Now's defences had held. The authorities' swift reaction had stopped the crisis in its tracks, and the new regulations would prevent anyone from trying again to profit from other people's future earnings. Eva was impressed.

'What a contrast to the comedy of errors that took place in the aftermath of 2020,' she remarked.

Iris, meanwhile, sank a little deeper into her melancholy.

Shaking the superflux is not enough

In the old days of our activist youth, few plays upset Iris like *King Lear*. I remember sitting next to her during a performance at the Old Vic theatre in London and, as the stage thundered with Lear's famous words of regret, noticing a single tear running down her cheek.

> Poor naked wretches, wheresoe'er you are,
> That bide the pelting of this pitiless storm,
> How shall your houseless heads and unfed sides,
> Your looped and windowed raggedness defend you
> From seasons such as these? O, I have ta'en
> Too little care of this! Take physic, pomp.
> Expose thyself to feel what wretches feel

That thou mayst shake the superflux to them,
And show the heavens more just.

When I asked her afterwards why the fallen king's epiphany
had touched her so, she got annoyed.

'What, that old fool?' she said. 'Who went all social
democratic on us when it was too late?'

'Well, if that's how you feel, yes, why the tear over a fool's
lament?' I asked.

Iris replied that it was the play, not the character, that had
got to her. It reminded her how the forces of evil never fail
to acknowledge and support each other, how effortlessly and
consciously they cooperate. Whereas the forces of good know
only how to betray and abandon each other when it matters
most. Hers was a tear of frustration – or so she claimed.

That Iris had no sympathy for Lear himself made
sense, for she had a deep aversion to the kind of paternalist
redistribution of excessive wealth – superflux – that he calls
for. She was of course all for reducing inequality, but she
feared that the kind of income redistribution practised by
Labour governments in the UK and various social democrats
in continental Europe in the 1970s would be short-lived and,
ultimately, counterproductive, simply providing capitalism
with the cover it needed to appropriate even more superflux
on behalf of an ever-decreasing circle of shareholders.

'Shaking the superflux,' I remember her saying that night
over post-show drinks, 'temporarily showed the heavens more
just – only to make them less so soon after.'

Never missing an opportunity to say, 'I told you so', Iris
began her reply to Siris's latest dispatch with a reminder of
their prescient opposition to such romantic notions and by

pointing out that in disempowering one set of spivs – the bankers – the OC rebellion had simple given cover to another.

Yes, she found the handling of the 2022 crisis by the Other Now's authorities laudable. Yes, it was impressive that they had done away with the absurdity of corporations owned by people who didn't work in them and not owned by those who did. And, yes, of course she approved of the end of abject poverty brought about by Legacy and Dividend. Nevertheless, none of this was sufficient to overcome her deep scepticism of Siris, Eve and Kosti's world. She remained profoundly suspicious of the Other Now's institutions, she said – of their capacity to prevent the environmental destruction that came with economic growth, for example, or of their ability to curb profiteering, as the Crunch of 2022 confirmed.

'Yes, bringing corporations and land and money under democratic control sounds splendid, but I just don't buy it: ending capitalism, and that alone, doesn't bring about a truly just society. Tell me, Siris, can you in all honesty say that it has?'

Siris's reply did little to persuade her. If anything, it did the opposite. The citizens' assemblies, she admitted, were imperfect. The OC rebels had aspired but failed to establish *isegoria* – the ancient Athenian ideal that every opinion in an assembly should be judged on its merits alone, rather than according to who spoke the words. Siris was also caustic about the rebels' claim that international solidarity had prevailed. 'The imperialist psyche, which rationalizes the suffering of its victims by treating them as "other", absolutely lives on,' she reported.

And even though Facebook, Cambridge Analytica and all the other surveillance capitalists were gone, technology was so ubiquitous and advanced that people still lived in constant fear of being watched, their behaviour monitored and policed if not by the NSA then by their own feminist comrades. 'The panopticon does not need capitalism to exist,' she wrote.

The one positive note in Siris's response was that meaningless work – the countless shitty, soul-destroying jobs people were forced to endure mainly so that governments could boast of their low unemployment rates – had been largely eradicated. 'The availability of a basic income for everyone and the democratization of corporations has forced us to invest in the automation of most chores, so the more dispiriting jobs simply don't exist any more.'

If Iris took heart from this news, she didn't let on. 'It's good to know that bad jobs are on the wane over there,' she said, 'but I bet their eradication did nothing to eliminate loneliness.'

What hid behind her stubborn negativity? Why could she not acknowledge the Other Now's successes, its proof that capitalism could be transcended, and that it could be done efficiently? Her dogged rejectionism surprised even her until, eventually, through her correspondence with Siris she realized what lay at its heart: an insurmountable belief that patriarchy and the market would continue to poison society even after capitalism is dust.

Freedom from the market

This was new to Iris. For decades she had raged against capitalism's total dependence on granting private property rights over land, buildings and machines to a minority who, as a result, had immense extractive power over the majority. As an anthropologist, she would tell her students that all societies featured markets, but they remained on the periphery of people's lives until the onset of capitalism. Before the eighteenth century there had been no such thing as a market for labour or a market for land. You were either a landowner or a peasant, and that was that. In the wake of capitalism, however, everything was for sale – not just labour and land but eventually even wombs, genes and minerals in outer space. Societies with markets became market societies, and every aspect of human endeavour was eventually channelled through one all-encompassing global marketplace. That's what made capitalism different – and a danger to our planet, to our souls, to our humanity.

When as an activist she was asked what needed to change, she would answer forcefully, 'Ban private ownership of land, buildings, machines – all the means by which we produce our material and spiritual goods.' She could now see that this was not enough. She had seen in the Other Now how the means of production could be ingeniously socialized and realized that she had been remiss: the problem was not just who owned what before entering into market exchanges. The problem was the market itself. It was the very principle of conditional rather than unconditional exchange: 'I shall give you an apple – *but only if* you give me an orange.' In the end, it was thanks to Esmeralda's Soho Address, her beautiful call for non-market reciprocity, that it finally dawned on Iris: she was more radical than she had realized!

After years spent cooped up in her Brighton sanctuary, effectively a market-free zone, exposure to the Other Now had radicalized her against the market society in all its forms, even the Other Now's post-capitalist one. Iris had come to feel that society's only saving grace was the rare and virtuous rebels who used their independence to embrace unconditional collaboration. The Other Now's reliance on markets jarred with her aspiration to live in a world where the good was sovereign, rather than the by-product of a smart market design. All of its achievements now seemed tainted and unappetizing.

The news of the Crunch of 2022 had been the catalyst. Siris's account of the scam devised by DCCS was the trigger.

'I bet,' Iris wrote, 'that the DCCS managers were men with no real unmet needs, except a hunger for power over the little people.'

Even with capitalism gone, as long as society privileges markets, Iris's virtuous rebels would be eaten alive by cunning operators always on the lookout for the next bargain. It gave her precisely the same sinking feeling she got from *King Lear*.

Iris did not dispute that the Other Now had shaken the superflux magnificently. But at what cost? At the cost of freeing markets from the shackles of the mega-firms' and mega-banks' monopoly. And why was this too high a price to pay? Because in her estimation, free markets, which may indeed require the end of capitalism to be fully realized, are not the solution. Markets, capitalist or otherwise, create the habitat in which patriarchy and oppressive power survive.

Her opposition to the Other Now, Iris concluded, was not dissimilar to her contempt for Lear. Just as a slight reduction of inequality in the name of social democracy only paved the way for a revival of inequality later on, so the Other Now had merely prolonged the reign of markets over societies – which is, of course, why Eva had warmed to it in the end.

As her exchanges with Siris drew to a close, Iris saw it all clearly. Her dream was freedom from, not of, the market – a dream that the Other Now dashed perhaps even more decisively than capitalism ever had. Was the Other Now's corpo-syndicalism not better than capitalism? Sure it was. But was it worth the candle if its outcome was a society in which Esmeralda, along with her Soho Address, could be snuffed out so easily?

8

The Reckoning Resumes

Digital toxoplasmosis

Thomas showed up at Costa's lab on Monday 3 November 2025. By then, Iris and Eva were exhausted, not only by their discoveries but by composing their own dispatches, describing Our Now since 2008, how capitalism in this period worked and how it had failed. After four months of this arduous back and forth, they had decided it was time to take stock and had agreed to dedicate a week to studying the dispatches separately during the day, before getting together in the evening to exchange notes. It was on the first day of their study week, as they called it, that Thomas joined them.

Though he had texted Eva a week earlier to confirm that he was coming, she had not been counting on it. Partly this was a way of managing her own expectations, so she was quietly overjoyed when he arrived, while also terrified that something might go wrong again between them. Painfully aware of his aversion to her shows of affection, she tried to not overwhelm him with questions and gave him plenty of space during the days that followed. The study week offered mother and son a nice buffer, providing the excuse they both needed. During the day, while Eva and Iris studied their dispatches, Thomas was free to do as he pleased, the four of them getting together at precisely seven o'clock every evening over dinners meticulously prepared by Costa.

Thomas chose to spend his days with Costa, intrigued by the weird Cretan's demeanour and fascinated by what his mother had implied about the lab next door – a place in which, as Eva had tantalizingly put it, 'all sorts of technological wonders lurk'. And Costa, it turned out, was the ideal companion for the troubled young man. After returning home to San Francisco, following his Brighton trip, a calm rage had gradually displaced hope in his soul, his initial excitement at discovering the Other Now being replaced with an obsession with keeping his equipment safe from Our Now's corporate raiders. Thomas felt comfortable around the broody, fragile and fierce middle-aged engineer. He appreciated that Costa never asked personal questions but instead would occasionally engage him in charmingly off-the-wall and unexpected conversations, alternately quirky and macabre. Thomas even managed to discover an interest in the preparation of Cretan food.

During one of their first mornings together, Thomas was playing a game on his tablet while Costa was preparing some lentils for the evening meal. Leaving them to soak in a mixture of water and balsamic vinegar, Costa turned to Thomas and out of the blue asked, 'Have you heard of toxoplasmosis?'

Thomas said he had not.

'Toxoplasmosis is a parasitic disease that rewires rodent brains in such a way that it reduces their fear of cats,' Costa explained. 'When the reckless mice are devoured, the parasite reproduces in the cats' intestines and then spreads through their faeces to infect more mice who in turn become vulnerable to cats. And so on.'

This guy is a complete weirdo, thought Thomas. *I like him.*

'I've been watching you,' continued Costa, 'playing that game on your tablet. You have the symptoms of digital toxoplasmosis painted all over your face.'

Thomas was more curious than offended.

'If I am the rodent,' he asked, playing along, 'then what's the parasite? And where are the cats?'

'I didn't mean that *you* are the rodent,' replied Costa. 'No, your *attention* is. Big tech gobbles it up through these games you play, while the invisible parasite breeds through their search engines and apps, making it harder and harder for you to hold on to your autonomy, to your capacity to direct your attention where *you* choose. Freed of fear of slavery, you surrender more and more to them.'

Thomas did not mind the insinuation that he was a mug, a plaything of big tech. In his conversations with his mother and with Iris there was always tension caused by the need on both sides to settle the matter and be proved right. Costa and Thomas got on because neither sought closure, let alone victory. Questions were posed for their own sake, claims were left unchallenged, differences were allowed to stay unresolved. For the first time, Thomas felt he could relax in the company of another soul, a genius even.

Costa felt comforted too. He basked in the long pauses during their strange conversations. He appreciated that he was not expected to fill them with insightful chatter. Eva had asked him to help ease her son's melancholy and loneliness by forging a connection with him, but soon it was Costa who was soothed by their time together. The freedom to punctuate silences with random thoughts messily articulated was oddly satisfying. It also gave glimpses of Thomas's mindset that would otherwise have remained hidden.

'I sometimes wonder,' Thomas ventured at one point, 'whether all of life is really just a fight for control, and because others are out to get the better of me, the only thing to do is to try to get the better of them first. Does that make me a freak?'

'Not as much of a freak as I am,' replied Costa. 'I sometimes worry that the whole thing is an illusion – that selfhood itself doesn't exist and that there is no "I" in my head that is me. But let's say for the sake of argument that you're right. That in this world it is impossible to prevent others from controlling you except by controlling them first. If I have learned anything,' he said solemnly, 'it is that to control others you must first acquire exorbitant power, and that, before you know it, such power takes you over and makes you its trophy.'

Thomas remained silent, processing Costa's observations.

'Suppose I could make your dreams come true,' Costa went on. 'Suppose you could press a button and be transported into a world where you control absolutely everyone and everything. A place where no one can put ideas or desires into your mind, but your desires determine literally everything about the world. A multiverse where you can not only do anything you want but you can do everything you want *all at once*. Would you press the button?'

Thomas had some questions of course, but having clarified the exact terms of Costa's thought experiment – which were of course the design features of HALPEVAM as originally conceived – his answer was unambiguous: 'Of course I would press it!'

Costa's moment of truth had arrived.

'Would you still press the button if there was no turning back?' he asked. 'If, once you are ensconced in that digital realm of unbounded pleasure, you could never come back?'

'Seriously, dude? I would be mad not to,' Thomas replied incredulously and without a second's thought.

Costa half-smiled and went back to soaking the rusks for that evening's *dakos* salad in olive oil and lemon juice. 'So much for the liberating power of for ever,' he murmured to himself.

Corona versus Crunch

On the Sunday evening at the end of their study week, the four of them met as planned for dinner in the mess hall, as Costa referred to his combined kitchen and dining space. Eva brought with her a chilled bottle of champagne, 'To celebrate the end of a fascinating week,' she said. Costa sensed that her celebratory mood had as much to do with her reunion with Thomas as with the insights they had shared from the Other Now. It was clear she was happy to be in his company again and to see fewer worry lines on his face, evidence that the week spent with Costa had had its desired effect.

Once they had moved from the bubbly to his *trahana* soup, accompanied by the obligatory glass of *raki*, Costa broached some unfortunate news. The wormhole had buckled, allowing for only tiny amounts of information to pass through. Communication with Kosti had been reduced to the occasional burst of Morse code, learned from their father, who had himself been taught it by a Kiwi soldier the family were hiding during the Nazi occupation of Crete.

'Is there no way to re-establish the wormhole?' asked Thomas, who looked up to Costa as to a genius capable of almost anything.

Costa explained that it had been a struggle to keep it open for as long as they had. To reopen it, he and Kosti were working on a drastic technique.

'By Wednesday we shall know if it works, though to tell you the truth it doesn't look good,' he admitted.

Iris reminded him that she was due to catch a flight back to England on the Thursday. 'I don't know about you folks,' she said, 'but I for one think it's time to head back home. I've been cooped up here all summer. Enough is enough!'

It was at this point that the conversation turned to the world-changing events five years earlier. Eva had been much preoccupied with the Other Now's Crunch of 2022 and how it compared to the 2020 lockdown crisis – and the economic depression that had followed in its wake. Those thoughts provided the tinder; Iris's final remark provided the spark. Naturally enough, the conversation began with a quarrel between the two of them, but once the topic of the lockdown took hold, it dominated the rest of their evening's dinner, with Costa and at times even Thomas taking the lead too.

'It's not the first time we've been cooped up together,' said Eva.

'Don't remind me, please!' retorted Iris.

'Remember, Iris,' Eva went on light-heartedly, 'how guilty I felt about coming next door for a glass of wine, while you were so blasé? And how anxious I was about doing so for months afterwards?'

'Yes,' Iris replied. 'In all honesty, I thought it pathetic.'

'Typical, isn't it?' said Eva. 'Whereas I was eager to comply with a sensible practice that the state should never have the right to impose, you supported the government's overreach while violating the very same ban whenever you felt like it.'

'Inconvenient laws are meant to be broken,' said Thomas. 'You weren't caught, so you did the right thing.'

Thomas's disturbing comment took both of them aback. Not wishing to cause a confrontation with her son, Eva steered the conversation in a different direction.

'Loath as I am to admit it, compared to the shambles our authorities made of the coronavirus, the Other Now's handling of their own economic crisis was outstanding. Admittedly, the Crunch of 2022 was a completely different kind of calamity, much closer to our crash of 2008. Nonetheless, I'm certain the Other Now's institutions would have handled a pandemic much better than ours did.'

It was the first time Iris and Costa had been made aware of Eva's extraordinary conversion. Shocked, they struggled at first to find the words.

'I … beg your pardon?' said Iris. 'What makes you say that?'

Eva gave a typical economist's reply.

'First off, consider their central banks,' she began. 'As every person and company has an account at their country's central bank, the bank can hand over a sum of money to everyone directly. No intermediaries, no laborious means testing, no questions asked, no forms to fill; some functionary just has to push a few buttons and every person suddenly has extra money to spend. In our situation, only the commercial banks have accounts at the central bank, so the only way it can refloat a collapsed economy is by giving money to them, hoping they will pass it on in the form of loans. But what do you always say the prime directive of a commercial bank is, Iris?'

'Never lend to anyone who actually needs the money,' Iris replied, reeling somewhat from being agreed with.

'Precisely. The moment you put a commercial bank between the central bank's money and the people out there, two things happen: much of it never gets to the people, and what does goes largely to those who don't need it. If we'd had the same central bank facility in 2020 as the Other Now had in 2022, we could have replaced all lost incomes and prevented most, if not all, bankruptcies immediately.'

The second depression-busting feature of the Other Now, Eva went on, was the absence of share markets. To Iris and Costa, who had witnessed Eva's initial outrage at that notion when she first encountered it in Brighton, this was a mind-boggling concession.

'Like a lot of people from my world,' Eva explained, 'to me 2008 was a wake-up call. From that point on, I grew increasingly concerned at the swelling disconnect between the real economy and the financial markets. But I remember how in 2020 that disconnect became a chasm. Even with half the world's population locked up, businesses failing everywhere, unemployment engulfing the planet, the stock markets were nonetheless doing nicely, thank you very much. Why? Because those loans made possible thanks to the largesse of central banks and governments went not to the people, as you say, but to the directors of big business, who promptly used them to buy back their own shares. That's why share prices shot up just as the real economies collapsed, and no doubt their bonuses shot up too as a result. They just couldn't lose. While everyone else suffered – including those big businesses – company directors and their bankers flourished.'

'You're telling me you've only just realized this?' asked Costa.

Eva confessed that before the wormhole afforded her a glimpse of alternative possibilities, she was simply unable to imagine a market society without banks or share markets. But now she could and it had made at least a few things very clear to her.

'The Other Now got this much right,' she said emphatically. 'In times of economic crisis, commercial banks and share markets wreck the central bank's capacity to help society mend itself and are nothing but a drag on a market economy.'

The third great advantage of the Other Now that Eva believed would have helped Our Now, had it had it, was the International Monetary Project, which could also have done for different countries and regions what the Other Now's central banks would have done for its residents. All the IMP had to do at a time of global crisis, she explained, was credit national accounts held at the IMP with different amounts of Kosmos reflecting the extent of the damage done to each country's economy.

'And if some weaker countries suffered permanent losses of factories, agriculture or tourist income,' she concluded, 'the trade-imbalance and surge-funding levies flowing into the International Redistribution and Development Depository would have compensated with the necessary long-term investment.'

'I tell you what else we could have done with in 2020,' Costa interjected. 'Their Sovereign Data Fund. The single most important advantage we humans have over any virus is that we can

– in theory – mount a coordinated global effort against it, provided we have the means and the desire. When it spreads globally, the virus in China can never share information with its counterparts in America or Africa. But we can! So, if we'd had the Other Now's open-source global data depository, think how much more quickly we could have tracked its course and developed a vaccine. We could have strangled the pandemic in its cradle.'

Jeff versus Akwesi

As Eva and Costa analysed the technical possibilities, Iris grew impatient. For her, things were simple.

'In Our Now, billions of humans were and still are one payday away from ruin. When the virus hit in 2020, it was simply exposed for all to see. Waiters, farmhands, caterers, cleaners, office workers, nurses, drivers and countless others lived hand to mouth, with barely anything in the bank to fall back on. The same went for small businesses operating on wafer-thin margins. One or two days without customers was enough for them to go under. All this talk of refloating the economy ignores the essential underlying problem. Do you remember, Eva, that article by Arundhati Roy you sent me from the *Financial Times* of all places?'

The lines Iris had in mind were transcribed in her diary:

> Historically, pandemics have forced humans to break with the past and imagine their world anew. This one is no different. It is a portal, a gateway between one world and the next. We can choose to walk through it, dragging the carcasses of our prejudice and hatred, our avarice, our data banks and dead ideas, our dead

rivers and smoky skies behind us. Or we can walk through lightly, with little luggage, ready to imagine another world.

'Remember, Eva,' she went on, 'how back in 2020 you were one of those who refused to imagine another world, continuing instead to drag along the carcasses of dead ideas?'

'Maybe you and people like you,' replied Eva, smiling, 'were the reason I refused to imagine that other world. Your collectivist fantasies and authoritarianism were what made them seem so dangerous. What irks you now – admit it, Iris – is that I have turned out to be more open, deep down, than you ever were to another world that actually answers your concerns while respecting the basic human liberties that I've always defended.'

From a young age Thomas had learned how to shut out the squabbling pair, as he called Iris and Eva. As far as he was concerned, society was a nasty, brutish place that only caused him heartache, and the pointlessness of their obsessive battling over the whys and wherefores of it only irked him. He had therefore remained silent, more interested in Costa's food than in Eva and Iris's debate. But to Costa, Thomas's absence from the conversation seemed unhealthy. He knew Thomas was generally more interested in the technicalities of the wormhole than in what lay at its other end, but in a bid to involve him in the conversation, Costa hit upon the one angle that he thought likely to capture the young man's imagination.

Before Iris had a chance to respond to Eva's challenge, Costa turned to Thomas and said, 'If you ask me, the most interesting difference between Our Now and theirs during our respective crises was to do with power.'

To Costa's satisfaction, Thomas's ears immediately pricked up.

'And if you want to understand what makes some people powerful and others pushovers,' he went on, 'then you need only compare the stories of Chris and Akwesi.'

Sensing that Costa had her son's attention, Eva signalled to Iris to keep quiet.

Costa began with the story of Chris Smalls, an Amazon employee who had dared organize a walkout from the company's Staten Island facility in protest at working conditions during the pandemic. He shot momentarily to fame when it was revealed that, having fired him, Amazon's ultra-rich and uber-powerful directors strategised on a teleconference how to direct the media's gaze upon Smalls in a manner that diminished him and his cause. But even though a considerable number of public figures spoke out in Chris's defence and decried Amazon's tactics, Costa explained, the furore had no effect. Amazon emerged from the 2020 lockdown richer, stronger and more influential than ever. As for Chris, once his five minutes of fame faded, he remained fired and vilified.

'It wasn't the first time a corporation had emerged from a global catastrophe stronger and with a splendid reputation among an appreciative public,' Costa said. 'At the end of the Second World War, Ford and General Motors were enshrined in American mythology as patriotic corporations that had helped defeat the Axis. For decades afterwards, if you claimed as some did that "What's good for General is good for America" you'd find plenty of Americans nodding in agreement. Could any corporation best this, you might wonder? Well, Amazon did in 2020.'

During the pandemic, Costa explained, while most companies were shedding jobs, putting thirty million Americans on the dole in a single month, Amazon bucked the trend and appeared to a swathe of Americans like a cross between the Red Cross, delivering essential parcels to confined citizens, and Roosevelt's New Deal, hiring one hundred thousand extra staff and paying them a couple of extra dollars an hour to boot. Of course, behind the façade, the reality that Chris Smalls protested against was grim: in its warehouses Amazon treated its human workers as fungible, expendable units reducible to their physical capacity to pick and pack. Good luck to anyone who protested at unhygienic facilities or a lack of protective equipment or low sick pay. That was the ugly reality behind Amazon's elevation from a near-monopoly to something closer to a state within a state.

'All power to Bezos!' said Thomas. 'If this Smalls guy couldn't hack it at Amazon, he should have left anyway. No one asked him to work there. If you can't take care of yourself, that's your lookout.'

Costa had expected – even hoped for – this reaction. He anticipated that Thomas would see Chris as a weakling whose sacrifice was an unavoidable corollary of Jeff Bezos's mesmerizing will to power. In fact, he sympathized with Thomas's inability to care about Amazon's ethics. How could it be otherwise for a young man overflowing so conspicuously with sadness and who felt as powerless as he did? The boy's yearning for power compelled him to admire and submit to it wherever he encountered it.

'Maybe so,' said Costa. 'But there's another kind of power – entirely different but equally overwhelming. More powerful than Amazon and Bezos, it turns out. And we can see it in the story of Akwesi and his Bladerunners.'

Costa described their Days of Inaction and the successes they had had in securing pay rises for the Amazon workforce, but Thomas remained sceptical.

'Bezos might have thrown them a bone to keep them quiet,' Thomas said, 'but I don't see how a bunch of consumers could ever weaken a megalith like Amazon enough to enable its takeover by the Chris Smalls of this world.'

'Power always rests on the law of large numbers,' Costa replied. 'No despot, oligarch or entrepreneur has enough power to rule millions without their tacit consent. The truth about despotic power lies not in the despot's weapons, bank accounts or computer servers but in the minds of those the despot controls. As long as the many believe they are powerless they remain so. In that sense, Bezos and Akwesi were not as different as you might think.

'The key to assembling immense power,' Costa went on, 'is to aggregate the tiny capacities of many, many people. Bezos did this slowly, gradually building up Amazon's overwhelming appeal as the path of least resistance for countless consumers, vendors and workers. All he needed was for millions to learn instinctively to think of Amazon whenever they wanted to buy a book or a gadget or any household item quickly. And, of course, he needed to keep prices low courtesy of an army of workers with no option but to accept robot-like, soul-destroying, low-paid warehouse jobs. Akwesi's army, by contrast, followed in the tiny footsteps of the Lilliputians who immobilized Gulliver.'

It was hard for little people to believe they had power, Costa explained. It took inspirational leadership to persuade them that they did, and then it took serious organization combined with smart strategizing for that belief to have any effect. Akwesi's strategy was to start small but aim high. His Bladerunners' Days of Inaction required of consumers only tiny sacrifices, but delivered confidence-boosting rewards. Not visiting a website for a day cost consumers next to nothing but, from the very start, thanks to Akwesi's global reach, it translated into large costs for corporations like Amazon. Immediately, the Lilliputians saw the effect they could have, and the Days of Inaction became opportunities for feeling part of an effective movement. Whereas previous protest movements took effort and commitment on the part of all involved, Akwesi's innovation, according to Costa, was to offer disheartened folks the chance to make a difference without personally sacrificing that much at all.

And in the same way that Bezos shored up Amazon by broadening its power base, from merely selling stuff over the Internet to cornering the market for cloud computing and expanding into artificial intelligence, so Akwesi's Bladerunners widened their power base by combining the Days of Inaction with the campaigns of Esmeralda's Crowdshorters and with those of the Solsourcers, the Environs and the rest of the OC rebels.

'Bezos and Akwesi were equally talented at amassing power,' Costa concluded. 'The basic difference was that Bezos used people power to milk people while Akwesi used it to empower them.'

Thomas had been listening intently. Costa inferred from his silence that he didn't quite know whether to be impressed or dismissive. Sensing his vacillation, Costa chose a different approach.

'Forget the politics and look at it aesthetically,' he suggested. 'The force assembled by Akwesi is more beautiful than the blunt and boring power of an ultra-rich man and his sycophantic henchmen. If you were to put the two forces to music, Bezos's would sound like Wagner's 'Ride of the Valkyries', Akwesi's like Beethoven's Ninth.'

As Thomas and Costa continued their discussion, Eva reflected on her son's character and the relationship that was taking shape before her. Costa's musical references had been lost on the young man, and he had been forced to attempt a different analogy. But had Thomas been familiar with the two musical works, Eva was sure he would have chosen the Valkyries every time. Beethoven's 'Ode to Joy' required an optimism of the spirit that her son lacked. She felt keenly that it was the absence of a father figure in his life that made him susceptible to absolutist patriarchal power. A Jeff Bezos, a Rupert Murdoch, a Darth Vader, especially a Mephistopheles, would find it easy to enlist Thomas in their enterprise, their boisterous validation of male power promising him what he had lacked all his life in a way that democratic power, however intellectually intriguing and aesthetically pleasing, could not. So, as she discerned faint signs that Costa was, in some small way, fulfilling Thomas's yearning for a *padre padrone*, even while he challenged that desire, she found herself holding back the tears.

Bleak 20s

While Eva understood Thomas's vulnerability to naked power in psychological terms, Costa saw it as an aspect of a wider political malaise that had taken hold in the last five years and shaped the young man's adolescent mind. Having secured Thomas's interest, he continued to press the point.

'You won't remember,' he said, 'having been so young at the time, but before 2020 politics in democratic countries was different. It was almost like a game, with the parties resembling teams who had good or bad days on the pitch, scoring or conceding points that propelled them up or down a league table which, at season's end, determined who got the ultimate prize: the opportunity to form a government – without of course really being in power. But then, all of a sudden, in 2020 the general feeling that politicians were not really in control gave way to the realization that governments everywhere – not just in China and Russia and authoritarian states, but the supposedly liberal ones too – possessed immense powers. With the arrival of the virus came the twenty-four-hour curfew, the closure of the local pub, the ban on walking through the park, the suspension of sport, the emptying of theatres, the silencing of music venues. All notions of a minimal state mindful of its limits and eager to cede power to individuals went out of the window. Many salivated at this show of raw state power. Even free-marketeers like Eva here, who had spent their lives shouting down any suggestion of even the most modest boost in public spending, demanded the sort of state control of the economy not seen since Leonid Brezhnev was running the Kremlin. Across the world, the state funded private firms' wage bills, renationalized utilities and took shares in airlines, car makers, even banks. From the first week of lockdown, the pandemic stripped away the veneer of politics to reveal the boorish reality underneath: that some people have the power to tell the rest what to do.'

'That's exactly what I mean,' said Thomas. 'If you don't control others, they will control you. It's inescapable.'

'Yes, in that sense you're right,' conceded Costa. 'As Lenin said, politics is about who does what to whom, nothing more. But what 2020 did not do, I'm sorry to say, is what some naïve leftists had hoped it might: revive state power as a power for good.'

'Not all of us were naïve, let me tell you,' interjected Iris. 'As I tried to remind those absurdly optimistic fools at the time, the right wing has never really been opposed to state power. Thatcher left the British state larger, more powerful and more concentrated than she found it. It was never about the village baker or the local butcher. Thatcherism grasped that an authoritarian state was needed to support markets controlled by corporations and banks. Why should they hesitate for a moment in 2008 or in 2020 to unleash massive government intervention to preserve that power? Those leftists fantasized about a renaissance of the commons, of public goods, of a new consensus on the common interest. They completely confused state power with people power. And besides, they forgot the essential lesson of the 1930s: economic depression is a breeding ground for political monsters.'

'Maybe you find it hard to imagine,' Costa continued, addressing Thomas, 'but the world you know, in which Amazon delivers everyone's groceries and might means right, did not always seem quite so inevitable. It was our failure to oppose the powerful – first in 2008 and then again in 2020 – that made it so. Believe me, we the people *gave* Bezos his power just as much as he won it from us. As Iris says, big business has always needed the state to impose and enforce the monopolies – on property, on resources, on funds, on markets – on which it relies. When we strengthened the state in response to the coronavirus, there was never a serious prospect that it would empower the chronically disempowered. Of course it was the Amazons of this world who benefited. Airlines took a while to return to the skies, true, but money soon resumed its speed-of-light travels across the planet, and all those lethal emissions that had temporarily subsided returned to choke the atmosphere just as they had before as production lines were restored and global trade resumed. Answer me this: who do you think suffered most during the coronavirus pandemic? Do you think it was America or China? Europe or Africa?'

'Wasn't the data inconclusive in the end? It turned out that none of it was reliable, I thought,' replied Thomas.

'You of all people should know: in all countries, on all continents, it was the weak who suffered most, as they always must. In 2020, the virus came for the British prime minister, the Prince of Wales, even Hollywood's nicest star. But they survived. It was the poorer and the browner people that the Grim Reaper actually claimed. Why? Just as Bezos's power was given to him, so these people's weakness was bestowed upon them by society. It was disempowerment that created their poverty, and it was poverty that aged them faster and made them more vulnerable to disease. And it was the widening gulf between these two groups of people, between the beneficiaries of lockdown – Amazon, Google, Netflix, Microsoft, their shareholders and financiers – and the billions who struggled and suffered in its aftermath that led to the monsters Iris was warning about who govern us now.'

Costa described to Thomas how the hellish cycle of mutual reinforcement between inequality and economic stagnation, so familiar in the aftermath of 2008, returned with a vengeance in the early 2020s. Instead of international cooperation, borders went up and the shutters came down. Nationalist leaders offered demoralized citizens a simple trade: authoritarian powers in return for protection from lethal viruses – and scheming dissidents.

'If cathedrals were the Middle Ages' architectural legacy,' Costa claimed, 'our 20s have so far contributed electrified fences and flocks of drones buzzing in their shadow. Finance and nationalism, already on the rise before 2020, have been the clear winners since. The great strength of these new fascists, though, is that unlike their forerunners a century ago, they never had to wear brown shirts or even enter government to gain power. The panicking establishment parties – the liberals and social democrats – have been falling over themselves to do their job for them through the power of big tech. It's only since we began living our lives in fear of infection that human rights have become an unaffordable luxury. The apps and bracelets with which governments now track our every move began, you may not realize, as a way of stopping new outbreaks. Systems designed to monitor coughs now also monitor laughs. It makes the KGB and Cambridge Analytica seem positively neolithic.'

Costa realized he had been speaking for some time now, and the good work he'd done by engaging Thomas was in danger of being undone.

'Cambridge who?' Thomas asked

By now dinner was finished and eyelids were starting to feel heavy from the champagne they had drunk and the *raki* that had followed it.

'Never mind, just another reminder that I'm part of ancient history,' replied Costa gently. He got up and began to tidy away the plates.

Rising slowly to head for bed, Eva said, 'It's true, the virus has held up a mirror to our collective face. At the time I didn't realize it. But now, I must say, I don't like what it revealed about us.'

Thirteen years after chance had brought them together, Iris and Eva were sounding alike for the first time. Impressed, Thomas asked them if encountering the Other Now together had been 'their moment of truth', opening the way to a rapprochement.

'Moments of truth are a fiction,' Iris said, adding, 'Truth grows organically, Thomas. There was never a particular moment or event that pushed my thinking and your mother's closer together. Epiphanies are an illusion that our minds conjure up to explain our failure to realize the obvious earlier.'

Amused, perhaps even a little moved that Iris should acknowledge their convergence, Eva said goodnight and quietly left for bed.

At the sink, Costa was busy with his elaborate washing-up routine, his mind at work on computations for how to restore the wormhole, but even so he had caught the drift of their conversation. Now he made the point that had been eating at him for years.

'Our moment of truth came in 2008,' he said. 'Once we dropped the ball back then, by 2020 it was too late.'

Yet again, though, Iris had to have the last word before also retiring for the night.

'Like epiphanies, the fork-in-the-road theory of history is a convenient lie,' she said. 'Yes, Costa, 2008 was a crisis whose wasting paved the way for the bigots and the financiers to prevail after 2020. But the truth is we face a fork in the road every day of our lives. Every single day we fail to take advantage of opportunities to change the course of history. And do you know how we console ourselves? We look into the past, pick out one "pivotal" moment and try to lessen our guilt by saying *that* was the moment we missed. No, mate. We miss pivotal moments every day, every hour, every freaking instant.'

Gently into the good night

It would be many more hours before either Thomas or Costa was ready to turn in. The night agreed with them, offering a peaceful backdrop for long silences punctuated by the odd exchange. With his mess hall spick and span, Costa sat at the table, transfixed by his laptop screen, which was filled with indecipherable mathematics. Thomas sat nearby, equally immersed in his game.

'There was something you said this morning,' Thomas said, breaking the silence. 'I can't get it out of my head.' Costa made no reply, so Thomas continued: 'That exorbitant power ultimately enslaves those who acquire it.'

'A fact that never stops them from doing whatever it takes to acquire it,' snapped back Costa.

The silence descended once more.

A little later, it was Costa's turn to break it. 'Perhaps this is a good moment to share something with you,' he said. 'My ongoing nightmare, you might call it. No one else knows this, but the corporates are on the verge of hacking HALPEVAM. It's inevitable now. A matter of days at most.'

Immediately, Costa wondered why he had opened up to Thomas, possibly putting him in harm's way. Maybe it was the realization that, for all his attempts to change the teenager's views, the two of them had something in common: they both knew what it was to crave complete power over others, and that knowledge caused them to dread it. Thomas foolishly wanted it to keep at bay the controlling power of others. Costa, equally foolishly, had sought the power to liberate humanity from the tyranny of manufactured desires. Is that not why he had built HALPEVAM, after all? Was it not a form of megalomania which, despite noble intentions, had given birth to a potential demon should it fall into the hands of big tech?

Thomas rewarded his trust. Unlike Iris and Eva, who tended to be dismissive of his fears, not to mention bored by them, the eighteen-year-old got it. He knew full well that big tech already held him hostage via the crude games he was addicted to. He could imagine all too easily what would happen if it got hold of HALPEVAM. Of course he would be first in line to join up, but he knew that big tech would extract a terrible price. The beauty of for ever would not be made available to customers. No, they would merely dip him into its multiverse of pleasures for a short while, just enough for him to crave more. Then they would pull him out and demand payment if he wanted to return. And they would do it again. And again. Until they had monetized the new technology to the full, their best customers simply being the last to be shattered by it, after which they would be committed to some asylum.

The mere thought of this made Thomas angry. And the more he thought about this, the angrier he became. If Costa were close to losing control of it, HALPEVAM would have to be destroyed. So too with the wormhole: big tech would charge substantial fees for access to one's self in the Other Now. In no time, the good people there would find themselves bombarded with missives from paying customers in Our Now.

Thomas knew very little about the world at the wormhole's end, but he had picked up enough to worry that such a barrage of messages would poison the Other Now permanently.

It took only a brief conversation with Thomas to confirm what Costa already knew: HALPEVAM had to be destroyed. He could not risk losing control over it. And, in any case, he was tired of living in fear. The only question was when.

He and Kosti had agreed to try to restore the wormhole the following Wednesday. Even if they succeeded, it might not be for long. Were a few extra days worth the risk? Should he destroy HALPEVAM here and now? Or wait until after Wednesday?

Thomas surprised him with his thoughtfulness.

'Is there something you've not asked Kosti that you need to? Something important Mum would want to learn from Eve, or Iris from Siris?'

Costa's heart filled with regret at how coy he had been in asking after Cleo, Kosti's daughter in the Other Now. Thomas was right: he needed the wormhole to stay open a little longer. And not just for himself. Thomas had the right to know about Agnes, his sister in the Other Now that Eva had not dared tell him about. A few more days of fear were a small price to pay for proper closure. 'Possibly,' he replied to Thomas, adding, 'I think Wednesday's experiment should proceed.' Thomas agreed.

What had begun, earlier that night, as a theoretical debate on watersheds and moments of truth had yielded a decision that, two days later, on Wednesday 12 November 2025, would produce their indisputable watershed, their moment of truth.

9

Exodus

Too well

The next three days were Thomas's happiest. Having sworn him to secrecy, Costa swiftly admitted Thomas into HALPEVAM's inner sanctum. There he felt cocooned in Costa's strange world, among the tangle of machinery that occupied the vast, brightly lit lab. It was the first place to hold his attention more effectively than the fantasy worlds he inhabited when gaming. That no one other than Costa had ever entered the lab before made him feel special.

Costa worked methodically, rapidly but unrushed, with a dignified sense of purpose. Thomas watched intently as the master moved from station to station, attaching new devices to existing ones, occasionally pausing to exchange Morse-coded messages with Kosti. Careful not to disturb him, Thomas bided his time and waited until Costa went to his coffee machine for a refill before asking, 'So, what exactly is the plan?'

'As the great Mike Tyson once put it,' Costa replied with a grin, 'everyone has a plan until they get punched in the face. That is, I'm sure, what HALPEVAM is thinking about my plan as I manipulate its entrails.'

Thomas envied Costa as much as he revered him. Gaming allowed Thomas the solitude he craved, but afforded him neither kudos nor self-esteem. Playing in someone else's universe was not the same as creating one. HALPEVAM was the laudable product of Costa's pristine seclusion. Just as it had been impossible for the Apostle John to feel lonely while manically writing the Book of Revelation in his Patmian cave, so Costa's lab work shielded him from the loneliness constantly afflicting Thomas.

Over his cup of coffee, Costa sought to temper the youth's admiration by sharing some of his darker thoughts. There were times, he confessed, when he feared that only a thin grey line separated him from the crazed adolescent locked up in his parents' garage planning the next high school massacre. During the years he had spent designing and building HALPEVAM in his self-made technological prison, to avert losing his mind he would spend four weeks every summer floating off the southern coast of Crete on a small wooden boat, offline, reading nothing but poetry.

'Why poetry?' asked Thomas.

'Because it's all we have to prevent our dreams turning into nightmares,' Costa replied.

A futurist since he had read Marinetti's 1909 *Futurist Manifesto* at a tender age, Costa's faith in the future started receding in 1976 – the year he heard his beloved Sex Pistols singing 'there's no future'. Since then he had walked a hopeful tightrope over an abyss filled with dreams of emancipation shattered by the alienating power of his technologies. HALPEVAM was to be his redemption, his special gift to humanity.

'Now look at me. I live in terror that it will fall into the hands of humanity's worst enemies. Even if we restore the wormhole,' he told Thomas emphatically, 'we must destroy the whole damned thing within a week.'

Sharing as much technical detail as Thomas could digest, Costa described the accident that had created the wormhole.

He explained how HALPEVAM relied on CREST, the wake of quanta from our lived experiences that Iris had called a river of life, and how he had built Cerberus to prevent big tech from tapping into it. But when he tested Cerberus' capacity to scramble tiny strands of CREST, the wormhole had appeared unexpectedly.

Never before had the young man felt a stronger sense of purpose. 'So, how do you plan to restore it now?' he asked.

Costa explained that to keep the wormhole open and relatively stable, a similar process would be needed but that it would have to be incredibly delicate and coordinated with precisely the same process at Kosti's end. He and Kosti had scheduled it to take place at 11 a.m. that Wednesday.

Iris was due to fly back to England the following day, but Eva's plans were vaguer.

'What's up with your mum? Do you know what her plans are?' Costa asked casually.

'She was pressurizing me to spend Thanksgiving with her and her mum in New York and got pretty upset when I told her I'm going back to my dad's before that. I didn't dare ask what her plans are now.'

Having no idea whether the wormhole restoration experiment would work, or maybe turn his building into a hole in the ground, Costa decided not to go out of his way to remind Iris and Eva about it. So when they mentioned going out on Wednesday morning, only the second time they would have left the building since they arrived in San Francisco, he encouraged them. Thomas agreed they should be told nothing until after the experiment. If the wormhole got an extra lease of life, there would still be time to offer his mother and Iris one last opportunity to communicate with Siris and Eve.

'And I think you better stay well clear of the building too,' said Costa. 'It would be best if you went out with them. And try to keep them away for as long as possible. Suggest lunch. They'll never say no to you.'

Thomas was disappointed but understood: there was no knowing what havoc the experiment might wreak.

And so, that Wednesday, at just after one in the afternoon, having spent an awkward morning walking along the waterfront with his mother and Iris before ending up at a restaurant, Thomas made his excuses to rush back, leaving the two of them to enjoy their lunch. He was immediately relieved to see that the building was still standing. Hurriedly he made his way upstairs to the lab.

From the mess hall, everything looked normal. So normal that he feared the experiment had not worked. He called Costa via the intercom, not daring to enter the lab uninvited. Costa eventually appeared, his face ashen.

'How did it go?' asked Thomas breathlessly.

'Too damned well,' said Costa, sitting down slowly on the bench. He leaned back and gazed at the ceiling, smiling faintly. 'Too damned well,' he said again, with a distinctly Cretan gesture of amazement.

Coming?

'What do you mean you crossed over?' Eva demanded to know incredulously.

It was as undeniable as it was unbelievable. Throughout the preceding weeks, Costa had shielded them from the technicalities involved. While Iris and Eva had to be within the vicinity of HALPEVAM in order to communicate with their other selves, Costa had taken care of the actual exchange of information, providing them with printed copies of incoming dispatches and converting their missives into an appropriate form for sending. They had no idea of the almost undetectable orifice appearing as a tiny blue dot on the wall behind HALPEVAM's transmuter array. And he had seen no reason to tell them that their dispatches were sent and received by pointing a microwave antenna at that minuscule blue point of light on that nondescript wall. Now, Costa had no option but to let them see for themselves what had replaced the blue dot.

At first sight, it was as if an artist had painted on the wall an uneven oval-shaped patch of black, about three metres across. Until you got closer and tried to touch it. Iris was reminded of a sculpture by Anish Kapoor, which used a perfectly black convex form to create the illusion of a black surface that one's hand would pass straight through if you tried to touch it. Thomas was the first to dare try; it was as if the wall weren't there. Frightened to see his finger disappearing, he pulled it straight back.

'Can you guess what's on the other side?' Costa asked expressionlessly.

They could. It was a portal to the Other Now.

'So, are you coming?' he pressed them. 'You have a little less than an hour to decide before it collapses for good. It's perfectly safe,' he added as casually as if he were suggesting a trip to the pub.

'How on earth do you know?' asked Eva.

'That's what I'm telling you: I've been through it. And as you can see, I came back. In one piece. But it won't stay open for much longer. So, make your minds up.'

Where to?

They sat around the dinner table for the last time, mugs of coffee in hand, struggling to absorb the news. In a mood better than any he had been in for years, Costa broke with tradition and put some music on. Iris noticed he had chosen Roxy Music's 'Both Ends Burning'. She would soon know why.

'Our coordinated attempt to stabilize the wormhole this morning,' Costa said good-humouredly, 'was, not to put too fine a point on it, a qualified disaster.' The trick, he explained, was to use Cerberus' technology at both ends simultaneously. The concept was sound and it worked. The wormhole was stabilized. Except, having nothing to base their input-output computations on, he and Kosti had miscalculated the aggregate energy release by a ridiculous factor. 'Both ends burning,' he admitted, 'my tiny blue wormhole grew into a black tunnel three metres wide.'

So, the wormhole had been made stable and expanded into a wormtunnel – but only for a very short while. The result was the brief window of opportunity that they now faced: to step through into the Other Now, if they wished, and live the rest of their lives there, or to choose Our Now, knowing that no such opportunity would ever arise again.

'Did you really cross over? Where did you end up? Did you speak to anyone?' Thomas asked hungrily.

Costa explained that he had spent a little less than an hour with Kosti in his lab. 'The tricky part was not going but getting back.' His passage to the Other Now was made possible by the presence of his own DNA at the other end – in the form of Kosti. How to make the return trip when they were both in the same place? 'To make sure I would end up back here, I left behind some of my DNA to function as a homing beacon.' Mistaking the expressions of amazement and shock on their faces for interest in the technicalities, he went on. 'If you must know, it was a jar of cotton buds soaked in my saliva.' Their expressions were not to be mistaken this time: he immediately realized he had overdone it.

'But how was it?' asked Thomas.

'A little like meeting a long-lost twin,' he said in an emotionally charged voice. But he hadn't met Eve or Siris, for the simple reason that Kosti had kept them well away that morning, just as he had Eva and Iris. But both of them would be there now, following Kosti's summons and the astonishing news of Costa's surprise visit. Their presence in Kosti's lab meant that if Eva and Iris were to jump through the black hole in the wall, they would end up there too.

'What about me?' asked Thomas, his mind racing. 'Is my doppelgänger also at Kosti's lab?'

Iris stole a glance at Eva, whose strained expression spoke volumes. Costa decided to explain the situation himself. Time was scarce, and what had to be said had to be said quickly. He broke the news calmly. 'No, Thomas,' he said. 'There is no you at Kosti's lab. In fact, there is no you in the Other Now at all, I'm afraid.'

Thomas looked dazed, trying to grasp the meaning of this information – and its implications.

'Eve chose a different path from me,' Eva said quietly. 'She has a daughter, Agnes.'

'So does that mean I can't go to the Other Now?' said Thomas urgently. 'What would happen if I just stepped into the wormhole?' Apparently, the news that he had never been born in the Other Now and that he had a sister of sorts mattered less to him.

'Yes,' said Eva turning to Costa with similar urgency, the realization dawning. 'What would happen?'

'Well', replied Costa 'if any living creature lacking a DNA counterpart at the other end were to step into the wormhole, then in theory Cerberus would detect a breach of security and destroy CREST, destroy HALPEVAM and presumably … destroy that person.'

Thomas went pale.

'Relax,' Costa continued, looking at Thomas reassuringly. 'Even though you lack a DNA counterpart, were you to cross over holding tightly on to someone *with* a DNA counterpart on the other side, you will end up safely there, your companion's DNA granting safe passage to both.'

'Isn't it a little irresponsible to be hypothesizing like this, with no evidence?' asked Eva anxiously.

'I have all the evidence we need, Eva,' replied Costa nonchalantly. 'We tested it with Baloo, Kosti's dog. On my way back I stepped first into the wormtunnel, followed by Kosti, who held Baloo in his arms to test our theory. Lo and behold, both made it here intact, Cerberus treating the Labrador simply as additional information. Then Kosti stepped right back into the wormtunnel, still holding Baloo. Both made it home safely, courtesy of a pile of DNA swabs he had left behind.'

Thomas's eyes lit up. 'Which means that I can come with you, Costa, right?' he asked, glancing at his mother.

The sovereignty of good

Iris intervened. 'Let me tell you a story from your past, Thomas. You were only ten at the time,' she said in her warmest voice, 'but it has remained with me ever since. And

I think, before any of us make any big decisions, it would be worth recounting now.'

Unsurpassed in the art of diverting a conversation, Iris had captured her companions' full attention.

'One evening back in Brighton, your mother came round in something of a state and asked me to look after you for a few hours so that she could go out by herself and clear her head. She seemed frazzled, almost despairing. When I asked what the trouble was she said that when she picked you up earlier that day from school, she had seen you punching a younger boy and then taking a toy car from him. She explained how she had tried to reprimand you for doing so but you had doggedly defended what you'd done. You told her there was nothing wrong with your behaviour, except that you'd been careless enough to get caught. All of your mum's attempts to convince you otherwise had come to nothing. She had tried to persuade you that, for their own sake, smart people renounce violence towards others, that it was in your own best interests to do so if you wanted to live a successful life. But her arguments had all crashed on the shoals of your brilliantly precocious reasoning. She was at her wits' end.

'I agreed to look after you,' Iris went on, 'and so your mother went out and you spent the evening with me. I probed a little, asking what had happened, and you explained your point of view. I must say,' she said, glancing at Thomas, 'that for a ten-year-old bully you were terribly impressive – and frightening! You rejected the idea that a successful life demands renouncing the right to be violent to others, to coerce them to do what suits you. You had a better idea, you claimed: learn how to appear *as if* you have renounced violence, so as to get others to relax around you, but be ready to pounce on them, to bully them, the moment it suits you – as long, of course, as you can do this without getting caught. In other words, to be successful learn the art of pretending to be good, strategically. Do you remember how I responded?'

Thomas admitted he hadn't the faintest memory of any of it.

'I told you the story of Odysseus and the Sirens – the mythical island-dwelling creatures whose mesmerizing song lured passing sailors to a beach, where they invariably butchered them. Like every enterprising man, Odysseus wanted to have his cake and eat it: to satisfy his burning desire to hear the Sirens' song but also to avoid being lured by it to his death. So he instructed his ship's crew to plug their ears with wax so they could not hear a sound then sail close to the island's shore but, first, tie him tightly to the ship's mast so that he could not succumb to temptation and join the Sirens. I remember you were intrigued by the story but, understandably, unclear what relevance Odysseus' story had to your quarrel with your mum. The answer I gave you then is the one I give you now: a good life requires that we find, like Odysseus, a strong mast to which to tie ourselves when it matters, lest we remain slaves to our every whim. This mast must be good and it must be self-chosen, but crucially it cannot simply be another, higher or more powerful desire. It must be something separate from and independent of our self. Lashing ourselves to it is the only way of ensuring the true freedom and autonomy that we crave.'

Costa suddenly understood what Iris was up to. This was her roundabout way of breaking to her friends the news that she was not planning to join them in the Other Now. And what better way to do this than via a rendition of her favourite theme: the sovereignty of good – her conviction that great art cannot be willed into existence by the calculus of an artist's desires; that, similarly, exquisite music and brilliant mathematical proofs emerge for their own sake, not because of a musician's or a mathematician's self-interested scheming. By lecturing Thomas on how freedom can only be built on rational self-restraint, she was working her way to announcing that she was staying put. A convoluted train of thought, but one that Costa saw through.

'Do you know what you asked me, Thomas, all those years ago?' Iris went on. 'You asked: how can my mast be made of something I don't want? It is the most important question of all. If one's mast is not to be made of one's own desires, then what is it to be made of? And my answer is this: it must be made of a capacity to do what is right, and to do it for no reason at all – except that it is right and good.'

'But how can it be reasonable to do something for no reason?' Thomas now asked. His unexpected comebacks always gave Eva a small thrill, who enjoyed being reminded of quite how smart her usually withdrawn son could sound.

'Animals and computers *always* have practical reasons for doing things,' retorted Iris. 'This is why they never do *great* things! To achieve true greatness, genuine freedom, you must be like the sculptor who sets aside her ego before chiselling a statue, surrendering fully to the feeling that she will go berserk unless she gives it form. Not being a bully is like a great work of art that you sweat long and hard to produce for no reason other than that you must. Just as art is, and can only be, an end in itself, so good things happen only for their own sake, for the hell of it – not because our desires drive them but only after we restrain those desires. Ironically, it is only then that our desires can be satisfied, as a by-product of our success in not being their slaves.'

For Iris, doing something for nothing was not merely possible but the prerequisite for a good life. Her subversive belief that reciprocity sucks, that life should not be lived on the basis of one quid pro quo after the next, was the reason she had been so moved by Esmeralda's Soho Address – and so devastated by the news of her violent death. For Esmeralda's words were a paean to the seditious idea that had motivated Iris since she was a girl: that love, happiness and freedom meant losing one's self in another, not merely exchanging or transacting with another.

It took only a small additional mental stride from lecturing Thomas to offering her friends an explanation of her difficult decision: 'The very things that the Other Now's laws and institutions have revived, protected and made great again – a world of transactions, of exchange values and of markets – are the very things I wish to escape. So why would I ever cross over to what sounds like my worst nightmare?'

Power to do what?

Listening to his difficult friend, Costa was reminded of one his favourite episodes of *Star Trek*. In it, the crew of the USS *Enterprise* chance upon a centuries-old spaceship in which they discover three cryogenically preserved humans. It transpires that in the early 1990s these three people had been suffering from incurable illnesses and had paid vast sums of money to be frozen and sent into space in the hope that, one day, they would be found, reanimated and cured by the advanced medicine of some alien species. Having been revived – and indeed cured – one of them, Ralph Offenhouse, formerly a rich industrialist, is informed by Captain Picard that he has been discovered by twenty-fourth-century humans living in a society in which technology provides for everyone's material needs. The accumulation of riches and possessions, which had so preoccupied the man throughout his life, is now considered infantile. The challenge is not to enrich oneself but to improve oneself. Mortified, Offenhouse tells Picard that he has it all wrong: 'It was never about possessions. It's about power.'

'Power to do what?' asks Picard.

'Power to control your life, your destiny,' Offenhouse replies.

Picard looks at him patronizingly and tells him, 'That type of control is an illusion.'

'I'm here, aren't I?' points out Offenhouse.

Costa recounted Picard's conversation with Offenhouse and then said to Iris, 'You're staying, and I bet this is why. Because in a true utopia, such as *Star Trek*'s twenty-fourth-century abundance-communism, Offenhouse's way of thinking has no place. But in the Other Now, it absolutely does.' Momentarily unsure of himself, he felt he had to ask, 'Am I right?'

'Yes,' said Iris. 'If your wormhole led to Picard's world, I'd leap through it without hesitation. But even though the Other Now is undoubtedly a far, far better place than ours in many respects, I refuse absolutely to go there.'

As a feminist freedom junkie, Iris knew the past was a horrible place, especially for women, but that was not a good reason to praise the present. Similarly, the hideousness of Our Now was not a good reason to leave for the Other Now, even if it constituted a remarkable improvement.

'I applaud Esmeralda, Akwesi, Eve, Ebo and the other OC rebels for eradicating capitalism, and I do not criticize them for preserving money and markets and those other financial instruments to get things done. Until we live in a world where material needs have been eliminated by *Star Trek* replicators on every wall, things like money and auctions will remain essential. Until that happens, the only alternative is the Soviet-like rationing system that vested horrid arbitrary power in the ugliest of bureaucrats.'

'But if, as you say, you think it a far, far better place, why would you not cross over to it?' asked Thomas.

'Because I prefer,' Iris answered, 'to stay in Our horrid Now than live in a much better version of it that only makes the prospect of a *Star Trek* communism feel further away.'

Iris was making the point that, once upon a time, she had disdained other leftists for making – that sometimes things have to get worse before they can get better, that improvements only hinder the generation of the forces that bring radical change.

'I did not waste my youth fighting against Thatcher's campaign to reduce all values to prices only in order to migrate now to a place where markets are even more stable, sustainable and admired – loved, even. When we reconfigure societies to put exchange at their centre, Thomas, we violate our nature. Humans thrived by hunting together, cooking communally, making music and telling stories around a blazing fire at night. Sure, the societies that replaced these communal practices with market exchanges unleashed great powers, allowing them to overwhelm others that did not. But there was a price to pay. Market exchange dissolves what makes us human. It is why our souls feel sick. By allowing exchange value to triumph over doing things together for their own sake – for the sheer hell of it – we end up crying ourselves to sleep at night. It's what depresses us and enriches the self-help gurus and big pharma. I am, I admit, fascinated, impressed, awestruck even, by what the OC rebels have achieved in the Other Now, particularly the democratization of corporations, money, land ownership and markets. Except that democratized markets still prioritize the transactional quid pro quo mentality that undermines the sovereignty of good and, ultimately, our fundamental well-being. Democratized market societies, freed from capitalism, are infinitely preferable to what we have here, except for one crucial thing: they entrench exchange value and thereby, I fear, make impossible a genuine revolution that leads to the final toppling of markets – and thus to the emergence of Picard's society, Costa. In any case,' she concluded more light-heartedly, 'anyone who believes that happiness lies elsewhere is a fool.'

Costa and Eva looked at each other. They required no telepathy to know what the other was thinking: that raging against the system was Iris's only way of being, her loneliness vaccine. The Other Now was too pleasant, too wholesome to rage against. It would have made Iris's life intolerable.

The crossing

'It is almost time,' said Costa. 'In less than fifteen minutes the wormhole will begin to lose its integrity. Iris, I think you have made your position clear.'

'You cross if you want,' she said pompously. 'The lady is not for crossing.'

'What about you, Eva?' asked Costa.

'Face it, Eva,' interjected Iris. 'You are the epitome of *Homo systemicus*, adapting to any system of authority and ready to do its bidding. If we lived in the Soviet Union you would be a party apparatchik while I languished in some gulag. Never a shrew, but entirely tamed, like Desdemona you preserve your purity by your complete submission to whichever system prevails. Your only saving grace is your love for this young man,' she said, looking at Thomas. 'It makes little difference to you if you stay or go. But crossing over will offer him his best chance of a decent life.'

Eva was appalled that she agreed with Iris. Were it not for Thomas, she would have been in two minds. The Other Now sounded fascinating, but Our Now had been kind to her too. Thomas was, however, the clincher. Being with Costa had, for the first time in years, brought him calmness and purpose. Crossing over would extract him from a world of pain, not least the monster that was his father. Moreover, over the preceding weeks Eva had begun to think of Eve as a sister and Ebo not just as a brother-in-law but as a force for good. And then there was Kosti, whom she was dying to meet, if only to compare and contrast him with Costa, Cleo and also Mari, Kosti's partner. Not to mention Siris, of course – heavens above, she would be losing one Iris to gain another, possibly a fiercer one! In the Other Now, Eva realized, she would have that which she lacked here: an extended family, including a half-sister for Thomas.

'Well, Costa, I will go if you will,' said Eva, knowing that if he went, Thomas would gladly follow.

It had also been clear to Costa that, from the moment he laid eyes on it, the teenager had been dying to dive through the wormtunnel – as long as Costa went first. Costa realized it was up to him, not Eva. Mother and son would cross over if he did, not otherwise. Like Iris, Costa also believed that the Other Now would be a better place for Thomas and so for Eva too. But how could he tell them he wasn't going? How could he extinguish their best hope of a worthwhile future by declaring his determination to stay to ensure HALPEVAM never fell into the bastards' hands?

That's when he decided to lie. Predicting that Thomas would only walk into the wormtunnel if he were to go in first, Costa played along.

'I shall step in first,' he told Eva and Thomas. 'You two follow me immediately. And, for heaven's sake, don't forget to hold hands tightly. OK?'

Anxiously, they promised to comply.

'What about HALPEVAM?' asked Thomas.

Costa explained that he had installed a failsafe device that would unleash an electromagnetic pulse so powerful that it would destroy every piece of technology in his lab once they had crossed over.

Thomas was delighted and instantly agreed. Eva felt she had no choice. Iris looked at Costa suspiciously for a while and then stood, bade all three of them a stern farewell and set off towards her room.

Thomas ran after her and threw his arms around her shoulders. Eva rose and made her way over to them. She hugged Thomas and then extended the embrace to include Iris as well. The three stood there for a long moment, tearless but all choked up.

Costa broke the silence. 'If we are to cross over, we have to go – right now.'

Eva and Thomas broke away from Iris. Costa looked Iris in the eye and said, 'See you.' Then he followed Eva and Thomas into the lab, closing the door behind him.

Eva and Thomas stood next to him, holding hands in readiness for the crossing as instructed. Costa smiled and walked casually into the perfect blackness on the wall. Eva and Thomas followed him immediately. The lab was suddenly empty and, but for the whirring machines, silent.

The madness of Hephaestus

Costa did not bother Iris that night. He had no idea if she had cottoned on to his plan to sneak back into Our Now, but by the time he emerged from his lab several hours later, there was no sound. He assumed she was asleep and went to bed quietly. He would save the ambush for the following morning – around 10 a.m., he thought, an hour before she was due to leave for the airport – giving them enough, but not too much, time together.

Iris betrayed no surprise when he appeared in the kitchen the following morning, where she sat drinking her coffee.

'It's impossible to destroy HALPEVAM safely from afar,' Costa ventured sheepishly. 'I have to do the job myself, in situ, thoroughly and over time.'

As Costa gave his explanations, Iris stared at him with an expression of sympathy mixed, unmistakably, with pity. Costa was, to her mind, merely the latest in a long line of male engineers who fantasized about breathing life into mechanical creations for some deluded higher purpose. Her list began with the Greek god of technology, Hephaestus, paused at Dr Frankenstein and ended with AI, or artificial idiocy as she called it. None of them had led to anything but ill in the end. *Goodness knows what horrors HALPEVAM will beget*, Iris had thought when Costa first explained his towering project to her. Her love for him, however, prevented her from sharing her thoughts.

And yet Iris's contempt for the defective sex was balanced to some degree by scorn for her own. She almost chuckled at the thought of Eva's equivalent inventions – the terrible economic models that Medusa-like turned the mind of any student who studied them to stone. Oh, how she would miss her! Iris's Brighton sanctuary had always offered her the essential freedoms – quiet and independence – that Virginia Woolf had argued were the prerequisites for any writer or artist. But that room of her own would be terribly lonely now that Eva was not on the far side of the wall.

Costa's explanations and self-justifications had by now morphed into his usual diatribe: the terrible uses that big tech would put his inventions to given half a chance, the importance of not leaving any trace of his blueprints online, his paranoia that, even if he destroyed HALPEVAM, 'they' could reconstruct it by reading his engrams, and so on.

Eventually she interrupted him. 'For you, dear Costa, I fear something altogether closer to home.'

'And what is that?' he asked.

'That your soul is too pure, too delicate, to bear the burden of having lied to young Thomas.'

Costa did not reply. But he knew Iris was right. His heart could withstand the solitude of his lab, the fear of big tech and the loneliness that Kosti's family had made him so aware of. But it could not also endure the weight of the lie he had spoken and acted upon so effortlessly. The thought of Thomas's disappointment broke his heart.

Iris's phone rang; her taxi had arrived. Costa helped carry her suitcase downstairs.

Accustomed to farewells, they went through the motions of pretending it was no big deal and of promising to be in touch soon. Costa stood on the pavement for a moment, watching as the car drove silently away, a poor substitute for the goodbye he would never be able to say to Eva and Thomas. And then he rushed back upstairs to get on with the elimination of any trace of HALPEVAM's existence.

No turning back

A month later, Costa put up his lab for sale. His work at an end, he intended to move to Crete permanently in the New Year. He was sixty-four. Not a bad age to retire. Maybe that wooden boat off the southern coast of the island could be his salvation again: a conduit to Another Now of his own, where his lying to Thomas might one day look nobler, less damning. Maybe he could coax Iris into visiting him, to reminisce about Eva, to imagine together how Thomas was flourishing in a world without banks, oligarchs or share markets. Then again, maybe not.

On the day he was supposed to fly to Athens, where he was to transfer to a domestic flight to Heraklion, he changed his mind. Instead, he caught a plane to London. The land of quiet desperation was better suited to his new project. It was not enough, he had decided, to wreck HALPEVAM. If he had been smart enough to tap into CREST, to build the damn thing, big tech could do it too. His duty now was to create gadgets that constantly sabotaged theirs. He would have to be careful, though. A fixed address of any sort would eventually be traceable. He would have to be permanently on the move, always one step ahead of them, dedicating his life to being their worst enemy.

Once the plane had taken off from San Francisco, he opened his laptop to pass the time. Unthinkingly, he created a new file and started typing. Ten hours later, as the plane was approaching Heathrow and the flight attendants asked him to stow his computer for landing, he found he had written a couple of chapters. Before switching off, he scrolled back to the first page to give the book a title: *The Madness of Hephaestus*. It would be a memoir.

Afterword

The Send button stared at me invitingly. Pressing it would end a year-long journey that felt like it had begun decades ago. One keystroke would have transmitted to Iris's publisher the book she had instructed me to write – the very one you have been kind enough to plough through, dear reader. But something wasn't right. Today is the anniversary of her funeral. It felt wrong to do so without first securing her blessing. And so it was that, earlier this afternoon, a red carnation in hand, I made my way to the cemetery.

The white marble headstone looked older than a year. I LIVED AS BEST I COULD, THEN I DIED read the blunt inscription that Iris had composed. I found it hard to accept that this simple slab, with this simple phrase carved on it, was enough for a person for whom a whole world, its alternate included, had proved insufficient. The thought of the red and black coffin rotting under my feet saddened me. As I laid the red carnation on her grave, its small splash of colour provided some comfort.

Stepping back, I looked around for the plane tree where a year ago I'd spotted Costa and walked over to it. Leaning against the tree, I turned for a last look at Iris's grave before heading home to rid myself of the burden she had placed on me. That's when I saw her. I was so startled to see Iris walking towards her own grave that it took me a few moments to notice Costa walking a couple of steps behind her.

Convinced I was losing it, I sat down, leaned back against the tree and waited for the hallucination to pass. It did not. Costa was carrying a bunch of red carnations. He caught up with Iris at the graveside and handed half of them to her. Side by side, they looked down at the grave, placed their carnations on top of mine and briefly held hands. Costa stood there like an ancient stele, while Iris leaned towards the headstone and ran her fingers across the inscription. I stood up, thinking I would make a run for the car park, but the rush of blood made me dizzy. Costa caught sight of me as I staggered and made his way to me.

'I knew it must be you,' he said. 'The carnation on the grave, I mean. How are you?'

Speechless, I walked slowly with him back to the graveside, where Iris still stood. She looked at me, squinting with puzzlement, until apparently to her complete surprise she recognized me.

'Yango? Can it be *you*? My god, it's so good to see you!'

'Iris?' I managed to whisper.

'Yes, my old friend, by golly how many decades has it been? You're looking well!'

Turning to Costa, I realized he was watching me, waiting to see when the penny would drop. Suddenly it did.

Relieved that I was not seeing a ghost, I grabbed his shoulders with both hands, stared into his eyes and demanded to know why he had not told me that Siris had followed him that night back into Our Now.

'It was all my idea,' Siris confessed. 'I asked him to keep it from both Iris and from you. And for goodness' sake,' she said, turning to Costa, 'have you been referring to me as … Siris?'

'It's just a nickname I came up with to avoid confusion,' Costa replied apologetically.

The three of us made our way to a nearby tea shop and when eventually we were all sat down and the tea had been poured, she proceeded to explain everything: how after the OC rebellion broke out, she had sold her Brighton home and made her way to New York to join the rebels; how Kosti had caught the first plane from San Francisco to join as well, putting the money he had made shorting Wall Street into the cause. 'As for Eva,' she added, 'we knew of her because of the work she had done for the OC rebellion, and eventually we made a point of meeting her well before the damned wormhole business opened Pandora's box.'

'By the way, we called her Eve!' I interjected.

Ignoring me, she went on to relate how eleven years ago she and Eve had received that extraordinary first summons from Kosti and had congregated at his lab, where to their astonishment they received their first dispatches from Eva and Iris. She described their disbelief on discovering that in another now – ours – Wall Street and the same clueless oligarchy remained in full control. Saddened and perplexed, they corresponded with their counterparts until, one day in November 2025, Kosti informed them that the wormhole had suddenly expanded and that the Other Costa had made a surprise visit.

'As soon as I heard, I dropped everything I was doing to go to Costa's – or rather Kosti's – lab to admire this so-called wormtunnel with my own eyes. Who should I find there but Eva – or Eve, if you insist – who had also been summoned. I should have guessed something else was afoot because Mari and Cleo were there too. While I was admiring the wormtunnel's pitch-black beauty, this Costa,' she said pointing to my friend, 'appears through it, scaring the living daylights

out of me. Moments later, it's Eva's turn to be stunned as her
strange-looking clone walks out of the wormtunnel, holding
on to a young man – Thomas, I presumed. While the two
Evas, Thomas, Cleo and Mari went next door to talk about
goodness knows what, I was left in the lab with my two Costas.
That's when this one,' pointing again at Costa, 'dropped the
bomb that he had only crossed over as a ruse – apparently
to get your Eva and her Thomas to follow him – and that he
was going straight back to destroy his lab. True to his word,
after coolly saying goodbye to my Costa, he looked at me,
grinned and walked calmly into the void. Without thinking,'
she concluded, 'I just followed him. When moments later I
appeared unannounced in his lab, he looked cross but said
nothing. After inspecting his instruments for a few minutes,
he looked at me again to say that we had just made it – the
wormhole had vanished.'

'But why? Why on earth would you do that?' I asked her.

'Surely if there is one thing you know about me, Yango,'
she replied cheerfully, 'it is that I am a dissident. There was
nothing for me on the other side to dissent from except their
political correctness and smugness at having created the
perfect society. All it took was one look at this man,' she said,
pointing at my dishevelled friend, 'and I knew what I had to
do – that I was more useful here.'

Costa had not been sure, she explained further, how to deal
with her sudden arrival in his lab but had insisted that she hide
there until after her counterpart had left for the airport. Then
together they hatched a plan. They agreed that she would keep
a low profile, that they would tell the other Iris nothing and
that they would go about their lives separately. Costa gave her
a sizeable sum of money and organized paperwork for her. She

adopted a different name and a different identity: Catherine Beaumont, a retired professor from some community college in Austin, Texas. They had stayed in touch, infrequently and carefully, to ensure the other was OK, but since Costa moved to England, they had hardly seen each other at all until now.

'Do you regret crossing over?' I asked.

'Hell no!' she replied with a tinge of American accent. 'This Now, my dear Yango, is my natural habitat – it's so bloody awful that I feel alive and usefully dangerous. Having experienced the OC rebellion and seen the institutions it created, I am more confident over here than anyone I know when lambasting the stupidity of the ruling class and its system. It is far easier to subvert them here, let me tell you!'

As she was telling her story, Costa had quietly excused himself to go to the 'restroom'. Through the window, I now caught sight of him outside the teashop, putting his helmet on, preparing for yet another disappearing act on his motorbike. She was not surprised. 'That's Costa for you,' she said. 'Drifting is now his way of being, a dreadful fact we must learn to respect.'

I nodded and in the brief silence that ensued took a good look at her. For the first time, I felt able to focus on her face without panicking about my mental equilibrium.

She looked back into my eyes, smiled, held my right hand in both of hers, and asked, 'And how are *you*, Yango?'

'Better than in many, many years, Iris,' I replied.

I was looking forward to the start of a brilliant old friendship.

Yango Varo, a few minutes before midnight
Saturday 28 July 2036

Index